WWW.826CHI.ORG

PUBLISHED MARCH 2008 BY 826CHI
COPYRIGHT © 2008 BY 826CHI
ALL RIGHTS RESERVED BY 826CHI

ISBN: 978-1-934750-03-2

PRINTED IN CANADA
BOOK DESIGN BY MOLLIE EDGAR
PHOTOGRAPHS BY GAIL REICH

ALL PROCEEDS FROM THE SALE OF THIS BOOK DIRECTLY
BENEFIT FREE STUDENT PROGRAMMING AT 826CHI.

THIS BOOK IS PRINTED ON PAPER WHICH CONTAINS
100% POST-CONSUMER WASTE FIBER.

826CHI
presents

RIGHT
IN FRONT
OF US

Forty-seven stories written by
Chicago high school students

* * *

Foreword by Alex Kotlowitz

CONTENTS

Alex Kotlowitz

FOREWORD

My mom drinks every day and has for the past eight years. She has a lot of stress in her life. When she is sober, she is a very smart, funny and sociable person.

There's a life packed into those three sentences. Francisca Cruz, who's 15, lets us know her mom is drunk most of the time, that she's trying to make sense of it, and that she imagines what could be. I picked out these particular lines, but frankly I could've done this with just about any story in this astonishing collection. I dare you. Open this book. Read a story. Any story. You'll be hooked. I was.

These writings will make you tremble—with anger, with sadness and with pride. They read like a collection of Raymond Carver short stories. Spare. Barebones, really. And, so intimate. So searingly honest. With these kids—all in their teens—there's nothing cute or predictable or, most surprisingly, self-involved in their writings. These authors just tell it like it is. No pandering. No punches pulled. No navel gazing. I picked up these stories one night, sat down on my living room couch and didn't rise until I was finished. I don't know that I've read anything quite like this before.

If the stories share one common theme it's the power of family—its power both to bolster the spirit as well as to tear it down. One writes lovingly of the new Gibson guitar—*solid black with fine yellow lining and a smooth rosewood neck*, the young author writes—given to him by his grandmother. Another writes of the exhilaration of graduating from eighth grade. But many of these students write of a parent's absence or a parent's misbehavior or a parent's dishonesty. One heartrending piece recounts the moment the author saw her dad kissing a woman who wasn't her mother. She was five years old. Trying to get out of the jam, the father tries to explain to his daughter that his lips are red because he'd been eating hot chips. She's not buying it. *I knew the truth*, she writes. *Donna always wears red lipstick.*

It'd be one thing if these pieces were just good yarns, but they're all so beautifully written. So direct, so straightforward, and told with such understatement and subtlety, like the 14-year-old girl, Estrella Nieves, who tells us that her dad's nickname for her is "mom"—a quiet way of letting us know of her responsibilities in the household. We learn that years ago her mother had left the family. One day, Nieves' dad brings her to meet her mom. *As the day went on, all I could think of was how she was not the mother I had dreamt of for years*, Nieves writes. *All I wanted was what every other girl wanted. I wanted a mother to make pigtails in my hair. I wanted her to brush my hair and tell me over and over that I was beautiful. I wanted her to tell me she loved me—and even though she could not take care of me, I wanted her to tell me that she wanted to.* And this is just where the story begins. These tales will surprise you. They take twists and turns that are unexpected, that are jarring, that feel, well, so real. You'll sense these kids' defiance, their hurt, their exuberance, their yearning to be heard.

All these kids wrote these pieces under the guidance of tutors at 826CHI. We need to figure out how they're doing it. Stories are our lifeblood. They're how we make sense of ourselves and of the world. These young authors instinctually know that. Their narratives will make you sit up and listen. You'll shake your head in wonderment at their eloquence. In one story, 15-year-old Javier Miranda ends his piece by letting us know, *I would write more, but I don't have enough ink, so I'm sorry.* We need more ink. Please.

INTRODUCTION

On our first day in Ms. Lockett's two English classes, Kait Steele, 826CHI's program coordinator, gained the trust of some fifty wary ninth graders the best way she knew how: by sharing her most embarrassing moment with them. She detailed how, in college, the combination of walking up limestone steps, wearing pajama pants and carrying a bowl of Brussels sprouts resulted in some impressive acrobatics as she fell down the stairs, landed splayed out on the ground, then quickly jumped to her feet and started directing people around the slippery mess of Brussels sprouts, air-traffic controller style. As she told her story, the students' guarded stares were replaced by intrigued attentiveness, and finally, uncontrollable laughter.

Kait went on to explain how this obviously amusing yet seemingly inconsequential moment was actually a major turning point for her, contributing to such important life decisions as transferring to a new university and seeking more joy in life.

More importantly, Kait used her story to get the students thinking about their own lives. "What are some life-changing moments in a person's life?" she asked. Birth and death, sweet sixteens and quinceñeras, new schools and new homes, the students called out. Then she asked the class to write down three specific times when their lives had changed. Many included those same events they had shared with the class; but some new, more personal moments emerged as well.

Students chose one topic from their list, and were encouraged to write as much as they could remember about that moment. Some students wrote about the birth of new family members; others, the death of a loved one. One wrote about finding out a sibling was adopted; others, about meeting a parent for the first time. Some talked about moving to a new house, and others, a new country. One wrote about ignoring the violence around her; another, about fighting a friend because they were in rival crews.

During the three months that followed, students worked one-on-one with 826CHI volunteers to make their pieces strong and to let their voices come through. They challenged themselves to add more details, bringing us closer to these particular days in their lives. Fourteen-year-old Angelica Troche brought us with her, to stand next to her after an apartment fire. She told us how "things seemed so far away—even things that were right in front of us."

Thanks to these students, things aren't quite so far away any more.

ACKNOWLEDGMENTS

To the 826CHI volunteers, we extend our heartfelt thanks. Lori Barrett, Mindy Bartholomae, Nicole Bock, Pat Carr, Wendy Hush, Susan Pogash, Mike Schramm and Cate White—you came to Aspira with an open mind and an eagerness to listen, and with that you encouraged and motivated the students. 826CHI's fall interns, Stephanie Clark, Carrie Colpitts, Paul Fermin, Adam Gaeddert, and Pat Mohr—you were invaluable through-out the process, working with the students, typing their pieces and help-ing in the editing process. 826CHI's spring interns, Nicolette Kittinger, Maya Marshall, and Libby Walker—we thank you for helping us prepare for the publication and release of the book.

For capturing the students' images that you will see alongside their stories, we are grateful to Gail Reich, a talented photographer. For their proofreading prowess, we are grateful to Janet Adamy, Staci Davidson, Kent Green, Sarah Jersild, Jennifer Johannesen, Lindsay Muscato, Tara Tidwell Cullen, and Andrew Yankech.

Alex Kotlowitz, it was an honor having you write the foreword to this book. You responded as openly and honestly to the students' work as they did to our prompt. Seeing their work through your eyes brought tears to ours.

Mollie Edgar, graphic designer extraordinaire, guided us through the process of choosing the visual theme, layout, and title of the book. Her creativity amazed us daily; but this was second to her greatest strength—her ability to draw a single theme directly from the voices of fifty students. Mollie, we thank you for your time, talents, and dedication to creating a book that reflected the ideas and words of its authors.

This book would not have been possible without the generosity of an anonymous donor. Thank you for giving the students the opportunity to become published authors; and for giving the public the opportunity to read these amazing stories. Your kindness will be remembered always, as these students proudly share their work for generations to come.

Thank you also to the 826CHI Board of Directors, Dave Eggers, Ninive Calegari, and the dedicated staff of the other 826 chapters, who offered support during critical times of the process.

To Kait Steele, 826CHI Program Coordinator, and Patrick Shaffner, 826CHI Outreach Coordinator—this book could not have happened without your tireless efforts and amazing talents. You make everything that happens at 826CHI possible.

Many thanks to Mary Rawlins and Jose Velazquez, administrators at ASPIRA Early College High School, for inviting us into your school; to Leslie Lockett, for welcoming us into your classroom; and most of all, to the students, for welcoming us into your lives. We hope that you've learned nearly as much from us as we have learned from you.

—*Mara Fuller O'Brien & Amanda Bruscino*
  Co-Directors, 826CHI

* * *

RIGHT
IN FRONT
OF US

Satchel Skoda

LIFE IN THE 'HOOD

Fifteen-year-old Satchel Skoda loves to box and to write. Most people describe him as unpredictable and funny. He can be mellow sometimes, and other times he can be quite energetic—even downright weird. Satchel also loves to sleep.

It didn't happen instantly. My mother always took care of me and my siblings. But somewhere along the line, I matured.

We're not the typical family. My mom came from Puerto Rico and had a lot of trouble in life. She says marrying my father was a big mistake. I always felt she had higher expectations for her children. My older sister was a normal girl. She always loved school and helped take care of us. My sister wanted to have a good life, which to her meant being successful and having a solid education. My brother is the one I really grew up with. We were very close—he was all that I had, and vice-versa. As youngsters, we did everything together and alike. That stopped as soon as he started getting older.

My family isn't perfect, but nobody's family is.

My father wasn't really there during my early years. As I got older, I started to notice what type of world I lived in. Instead of big, expensive houses, clean streets, and nice quiet neighbors, my neighborhood had a lot of government housing buildings, a couple of flats, and then there were some ordinary houses. Yes, there was cut grass in some yards, but there were graffiti tags on the sidewalks to grab your attention. My house was a little red brick one with a sign that said "Hispanic Housing." We even had to put up a big fence to try to keep people from running through our gangway, but it was made a little too late. Expensive cars were found parked in front of a businessman's house or in front of a hustler's house. You heard car alarms, sirens, shattering glass, *bang! bang!*, and parties with loud music in my neighborhood. Then there were those days when it was too quiet on my block. Silence was no better than those loud, dangerous sounds. Quiet days were scary days.

It tore me apart that my dad was who he was. Every birthday I had, he was in jail. I started to see and learn more about my neighborhood. Things are so different when you're a little kid who doesn't know about his surroundings. I knew that my mother was independent and that we were always tight on money. My family had a reputation, although I didn't know what kind until recently. I was always looked at as if I was a "Skoda"—my last name.

There were so many problems to worry about when I got older. I started to look at life differently. Since I lived in "the 'hood," drugs, money, and violence played a big role. My mother always tried to isolate my brother and me from those things, but it is really hard if there's nothing but that right in front of you.

I grew up really close to my brother, and he knew more about life than I did. My dad and half-brothers, who I considered blood brothers, were into the gang lifestyle, so we learned right from wrong from them.

As I got older, things changed. We moved. People treated us differently. Some people didn't like us, and others treated us like family. At times, we weren't wanted in our new neighborhood because we were from "the other side." Recognizing violence, seeing and hearing gunshots, and watching people throwing gang signs at my brothers and me tripped me out. When I was still young I was considered to be like my family, doing the same things as they did.

One time, one of my older brothers got shot. Everything went crazy. I heard rumors that he was dead. Someone told me "they" said I had gotten shot instead of my older brother. The shooting made my neighborhood even more dangerous for me.

Then there were times when I got shot at. Mistake or not, it was scary. One day, I was playing around with my brother and he chased me into our alley with the water hose. When I looked to the side, I saw a guy with a gun ready to shoot. *Bang! Bang! Bang!* It was so close that all I heard was the bullets ripping through the air. I felt them go right by me.

A couple months later, when I was on my bike, I guess I went into the wrong neighborhood. I had come from playing baseball, and I tried to take a shortcut to my house, so I rode fast and waited for my brother to catch up. When I went around the "round-about"—a big circle in the middle of the street with a yield sign—I saw a couple guys throwing up signs and they started to shoot. It was a miracle that I didn't get hit. Right after I passed the yield sign, a bullet went through it. I had been only a couple centimeters away from it. I have to watch my back and my family's all the time, because anything could happen.

As most kids do, I have my friends and we chill all the time, but we can be misinterpreted as "bad" or "not a person to be around." In Maplewood Park, my local park, we get stopped and checked by the police all the time, even if we are not doing anything. Things can go down for no reason—fights, shouting, police—crooked or violent. It happens all the time.

Where I'm from, it's hard to be successful and stay out of the typical "'hood life," but I don't plan to be there forever. I know I'm not the best-behaved kid, and I do many stupid things to get myself in trouble, but I think there's a time for everything. I learn from my mistakes. It's hard to stick around and to not get caught up in school. I try to lead myself in the right direction. I could write a book about the graphic things I've seen. Living the lifestyle and growing up in the 'hood isn't the easiest way to have a good life, but a lot of people do make an effort to change. I am one of those people.

Mariana Argueta

THE BEST OF BOTH WORLDS

"I represent my nationality to the fullest," says fifteen-year-old Mariana Argueta, who likes to be called Mari. Down-to-earth and a lover of music and dance, she also gives great advice to her friends.

I was born in Chicago, but when I was five months old, my mom sent my seven-year-old brother and me to stay with my grandma in Guatemala because my mom was working and couldn't take care of us. In Guatemala, we lived in the small town of Quetzaltenango, where I had a lot of freedom and it never got cold. Guatemala is hot and beautiful, and it is famous for the quetzal, a green bird with a very long tail.

By the time I turned seven, my mom had gotten a house and wanted us to come live with her in the United States. I didn't want to move. I was comfortable with my grandma, and I didn't know my mom. My grandma reassured me that it would be great in the U.S.; I would live with my mom and go to school there. It would be both exciting and scary.

When I arrived in Chicago, it was dark outside. I looked out the airplane window and saw all of the lights. I felt nervous because everything looked so different. The city was huge! My mom and step-dad picked us up from the airport. When I saw my mom, I started crying because I didn't remember her, and I had never met the guy before. I was scared.

My step-dad drove us to our new home. There were so many emotions, so many questions. My new home was an apartment, yellow and close to a big mall. My mom showed me around and explained who was living there: herself, my step-dad, one of my aunts and one of my mom's cousins. She showed me the room my brother and I would share. It was big and white, with a bunch of Disney characters on my side and sports posters on my brother's side. In Guatemala, I had shared a room with my Aunt Carmen. It had been of medium size with brick walls, lots of pictures of family members, and a cross in the middle. Although my first night in Chicago was scary, I felt safe with my brother in the room.

I had to adjust to many changes when I came to Chicago. When it snowed, the city looked like you had just opened a freezer. It never snowed in Guatemala; it never even got cold. The food here was different, too— there were some foods, such as McDonald's and pizza, that you only see in Guatemala once in a while. In Chicago, McDonald's was everywhere, and lots of restaurants sold pizza.

I also had to learn English because I was used to speaking in Spanish. Learning a new language was really hard. I felt really lost. I had to go to a new school and make new friends. Making new friends was a challenge because not everyone spoke Spanish. I felt really weird not understanding what people were saying. Coming to the United States was a big, dramatic change, but I had to adjust. And I did.

I have not gone back to Guatemala yet, but I will return for two weeks this winter break. I am excited to see my grandma, and at the same time nervous, because it is going to look different to me. I appreciate the fact that I started out my life in Guatemala. I now have a strong sense of both countries—their customs, traditions, and ways of life. I wouldn't have gotten to know my grandma if I had stayed with my mother. Even though it was difficult to adjust to the move, I feel I now have the best of both worlds.

Alexis Mondragon

KICKING BAD HABITS

People call fifteen-year-old Alexis Mondragon "Curly," after his curly hair.
He loves to play soccer and hang out with his friends. He assures
you that although he got in big trouble in fourth grade, now he is good.
He wishes he was allowed to chew gum in class.

When I was eleven years old, I would always get into trouble in school. I was so bad. My teacher would send me to the office because I always cursed her out. One day, I brought a knife onto school property. There was a fight scheduled for after school with the softball players because some of them were in a gang. I brought the knife because my friend gave it to me earlier to hold and asked me to give it to him when they started fighting. When my friend gave me the knife, I felt scared—I knew if I got caught I would have to pay the consequences. But I still had to do it for him; he was a brother to me, and he would have helped me out if I had asked him to.

When I came back to school the next day, I found out that a teacher had seen me holding the knife the day before. She had told the principal. The two of them threatened to "do it the hard way" if I didn't tell them why I brought it—that meant they were going to call the cops. So I told them why I had the knife. I told them about my friend's request. The principal suspended me for ten days, and my dad punished me. I couldn't watch TV or go outside for two months. It was the lowest point of my life.

For two whole months, I sat in my room. I did all of my schoolwork. When my suspension ended, my principal let me try out for soccer one Friday after school. I went with my friend Eduardo. We had to run, kick the ball, pass the ball, and scrimmage so the coach could see who was good. The next day, the coach posted a list next to the gym, noting who had made the team. That list was divided into two columns: the players who made the team on the left, and those who didn't on the right.

After school, I ran to see if I made the team. I wanted to be the first one to see the list. On my way to the list, many thoughts passed through my head. I wondered if I made the team. If I didn't make it, I was going to be angry; it would make my year even worse. I pictured my friends teasing me and calling me a failure. I really didn't want that to happen. When I reached the list, I saw that my name was in the left column. I was so relieved.

Soccer has since changed my life. Before, when I wasn't playing soccer, I was getting into trouble. Now I come straight home because I'm hungry after practice. I listen to my mom. I clean the house and help her out. When I go to school I work harder. I still play around in class sometimes, but I try to do all my work. I usually don't curse the teachers anymore. I changed in these ways because I had to—if I didn't, my principal said, I wouldn't be able to play soccer or compete on any teams. I also use soccer as my anti-drug and my anti-trouble. It really helps me focus on other things than the bad things I used to do. I would do anything for soccer. Soccer is my life.

Nayeli Guerrero

MY MISSION

Fifteen-year-old Nayeli Guerrero loves dolphins and wants to become a dermatologist. She loves giving advice to her friends, and spends most of her time dancing, singing, reading, listening to music, and watching movies. Two of her favorite sports are volleyball and soccer. Her greatest wish is to travel around the world. She describes herself as "nice, helpful, smart, crazy, and lovable."

As I cried in my room with my door closed, I listened to all the loud voices screaming. My sisters were crying, and chairs were all over the place. *God, I can't stand this anymore*, I thought.

When I was ten years old, I thought my future would be horrible. I had no one to talk to about what was going on with me. I was feeling bad about myself and depressed and stressed. My dad was drinking, and when he got mad he would throw chairs and my mom would scream. Girls at school did not accept me and made fun of me for having family problems. I thought my family would be destroyed. I thought my parents would divorce and that my sisters and I would be split up. I wondered why God didn't let me die when I was in my mother's womb and she was in a terrible car accident. The doctors had said I would not make it. Sometimes I thought God should have let me die.

One Sunday, one of my friends invited me to go to church with her. It was my eleventh birthday, and the person who led the youth service gave me a book as a gift. It was called *Planned for God's Pleasure*. That day when I went home, the first thing I did was open the book. It was small, and I finished it quickly.

Until that time, I didn't think I had a purpose in life. I wondered: Why do I exist? Why am I here? What is my purpose? These were the fundamental questions I thought about, and I did not know where to turn for an answer. My own family didn't practice any religion. Without these answers, I brought negative thoughts into my head.

As soon as I read the first page of the book, one of the most important questions was answered: Why do I exist? I learned that I had a mission and a purpose to accomplish something in life. I should not give up even though I had been through hard circumstances. I should keep going and try my best.

I realized at that moment that the very fact that I am alive means God has a purpose for my life. I wasn't created for just one purpose, but I was created for five special reasons. Like the title says, I was planned for God's pleasure. God did not need people to love him—He didn't feel lonely—but He needed to love people. I was formed for making a family. I was created to become like Christ. I was shaped for serving God. Lastly, I was made for a mission. This little book helped me understand why I'm alive, why I go through difficult circumstances, and what God planned for me to do with my life.

Life started changing after that. I started going to church and accepted the Lord as my Savior. I had never had a conversation about religion with my dad before now. I asked him to listen to me. At first he refused. I started yelling at him, telling him, "When will you ever have time for me?" Finally he sat down, and I explained to him how sad I felt watching him and my mom always arguing. "Dad, you may think I am crazy," I said, "but there is this awesome feeling in my heart that I have never felt before. It feels like I came out of death to a new life. Are you thankful that God gave me a life? If it wasn't for Him I wouldn't be here, talking to you right now. I realize that I am not alone. Even though I cannot see God, I can feel Him next to me." There was a big silence. "Dad, I want you to understand," I continued. "You think it does not hurt me when you and Mom are fighting. What happened to that promise to love and honor your wife?"

It hurt him when I started reminding him about the times he used to tell me, when I was a little girl, that it was bad to smoke and drink. He became really quiet. So I explained to him how this book had changed my thoughts and that it could also help him change his. I hoped it would help him stop drinking and smoking and help him be more respectful to my mom. After the conversation, I saw a tear in his eye and he gave me a hug—our first hug in a long time.

Since then, my dad has continued to go to church with us and once a week we have family time and talk.

I am glad that this book has changed my life in different ways. Not only the book, but God who put me in this world for a mission: a mission where I can talk about the word of God.

Javier Miranda

AN UNEXPECTED MIRACLE

Fifteen-year-old Javier Miranda speaks five languages. He is a musician who
plays Latino percussion, flute, clarinet, bass, guitar, and trumpet. He has
also been singing for almost ten years. He looks up to his sister Jessica, who
"has been working hard to get where she is today." He thanks his parents and
his brothers for helping him "resist these years of problems," and says he
wouldn't be the person he is today without them. He also thanks friends Apryl
and Jesenia for being there for him. Most of all, he thanks God: "If it wasn't
for Him, I wouldn't be here today."

It was June 11, 2005, and I had finally gotten to audition to play the flute in the Merit School of Music. I was so excited because if I got in I would be in the school orchestra, which has some of the best music players in the city of Chicago. My father drove us all the way there while my mother was sleeping like a doll. Immediately after we arrived, my audition started; but then my mother started getting these weird headaches. My father was worried, and so we left early. I was disappointed, but the health of my family always comes first. We took her home and took care of her until she felt better.

Later that day, my brother Tito asked my mom if we could go to the HIP, which is a huge mall on Harlem and Irving Park. My mom was bored, so she said, "Sure." While driving, she started daydreaming. We snapped her out of it because she almost ran a red light and had to slam on the brakes. We were so scared that she'd do it again, so my brother said, "You know what, Ma? I think I should drive. You just rest." As we were walking through the mall, she stopped suddenly and said, "What is this place? Where am I?" We told her where she was and she snapped out of it. She was okay the rest of the day.

The next day was my big brother Jose's wedding. We were all so happy for him, and everything was going great until it came time to give the speeches. When it was mom's turn, she stood up and spoke English with an accent we'd never heard. While speaking, she became dizzy and said, "I've got a big headache." She collapsed on the floor and instantly went into a coma. The ambulance arrived in a flash. They took her to St. Francis, but they told us they didn't have the equipment to help her because her aneurysm had busted. She had suffered a stroke. I was so broken down. I didn't know what to do.

Two months after the wedding, she finally came home. Her hair was shaved and she couldn't even walk. It was depressing for me, but I know God saved her from death and I thank Him for bringing my mother back with an unexpected miracle. Those two months were really hard for me, and my grades suffered. Now she walks, she speaks, and she does every-thing with ease.

I would write more, but I don't have enough ink, so I'm sorry. I'm glad my mother has lived two more years for the honor and glory of God. She means so much to me, and I don't know what would've happened if she had gone away.

Brenda Chavez

ZURY, LOOK UP TO ME

*Though fourteen-year-old Brenda Chavez was born in Chicago, her parents hail
from Mexico. A self-described MySpace addict, Brenda is a lover of soccer,
dance, and the Bachata music genre. Deeply committed to authenticity, she hates
people who try to be something they're not. Brenda can often be found
on the phone or spending quality time with her parents and two brothers.*

B efore Zury was born, I never achieved my goals. I was satisfied with
average and gave up easily. When something was going bad, I just
gave up. That was how my life was.

About a month ago, I joined a crew that my friends were a part of. In
order for most girls to join, they had to let the crew give them a beating
for ten seconds. I was lucky to go in without the beating. I watched while
other girls were getting hit to get in.

Here's how a crew works: If one of the girls from your crew has a
problem with another girl, the two of them fight and you are supposed to
jump in and help your girl fight even if you don't want to. That is the
whole point of being in a crew—somebody has your back.

One day at school, one of the girls in my crew got in a fight with another girl and I was the only girl from the crew around. I was faced with a problem. I didn't want to jump in. I didn't want to fight. I didn't want to risk suspension for something as pointless as fighting. After that incident, the girl was angry with me because I didn't step in. I didn't know what to say to her when she approached me. One week later I left the crew.

I joined the crew because I thought they were going to protect me when something was going wrong. I thought they were going to listen to my problems and try to help me out. My first week in the crew, I noticed how stupid I was for joining. One of the things I realized was, what if I get shot and never get to see my baby niece, Zury, grow up? I didn't want my niece to follow the same example. I wanted her to be something in life, so why shouldn't I show her how to do it? That's why I got out of the crew.

When Zury was born I realized that I had somebody that would someday look up to me. I made a promise to myself that I was going to pay more attention in school, think less about boys, and achieve all of my goals, even if they seemed hard. My niece has become somebody really special in my life. She's my little girl and I want to show her how much I love her by trying to be a good example for her.

I love my niece and I want her to say when she gets older, "Oh, that's my aunt, and she's somebody I admire, and I want to be like her when I grow up." The only way she would say that is if I have a good job that I enjoy, if I'm cool with her, give her good advice, and if I do everything that I propose myself. One way that I would have a good job would be by

26

studying and having good grades so I can have a career in cosmetics and be a professional dancer.

One day, at my house, I put music on and I started dancing. Zury saw me dancing and she started dancing too, and I just started laughing. She was nine months old. When she started walking a month later, she started dancing even more. I noticed that she does everything she sees, so in front of her I need to be a positive example. My brother was this example for me. When I watched him dance I felt like telling everybody, "Oh, that's my brother." I showed off but not in a conceited way. I just felt proud of my brother and I want Zury to feel the same about me.

If one day she reads this, I want her to know that she changed my life, and she's always going to be my little girl. I love her. Better than a crew, your family will always have your back.

Amber Forbes

GRANDMOM

Amber Forbes is a very sensible, down-to-earth fifteen-year-old who, thanks to her youthful spirit, people often mistaken for a twelve- or thirteen-year-old. A great dancer and sketch artist, Amber draws much inspiration from Tyra Banks because "she is a hard worker and has accomplished so much in her life." Amber is a great comedian and an even greater friend.

My grandmother and I were like two peas in a pod. She was a very kind, sweet lady. She rarely raised her voice at anyone. She never spoiled me with material things, like my mom does—and that's what I loved about her.

My grandmother was always there for me, ever since I was little. When I was two or three, my grandmother had a cat named Spider. I was so allergic to Spider's fur. When I got it in my throat, my nose, and my eyes, I would cough and rub my eyes until they turned red. My grandmother would stay up with me through the night.

My grandmother was strong. We were buddies. I used to go over to her house every weekend. She was tough—in a good way. I was her grandbaby. She was a trustworthy and faithful woman. Nothing could stop me from seeing her. She meant the world to me. We used to go to the beach, to church; it didn't matter where we went, as long as I was with her. We hung out all the time.

I remember my grandmother always defending me. One time, I wanted to go to a concert because I had never been to one before. My mom wouldn't let me go, which made me mad. I called my grandmom and told her what had happened. That caused my mom to go off on me because she was upset with me for talking about the concert situation with my grandmom. My grandmom called my mom; after they talked, my mom apologized, and I wasn't upset anymore. I have many of these special memories of my grandmother.

It was January 21, 2006, when my grandmother, Joan Forbes, passed away. I did not handle it well. But who does handle such a thing well— the loss of a very close relative? She had been out of the hospital for about a week when it happened. I had been at her house with my mom on Monday, earlier that week. She was wearing an oxygen mask to help her breathe. I was worried about her, so I stayed through the night. Wednesday came, and my mom made me go to school. As I was getting ready to leave, my grandmother told me I looked cute, and that she hoped I would be careful getting on the bus. Then I left.

On Saturday, my mom was still over at my grandmother's house. My sister and my cousin Keisha were getting ready to go over there, so I asked, "Can I come?" Everybody said, "No, no kids can come." And I wondered why. *She would have loved to see me,* I thought.

That night, my cousins and I were chilling at our house. I called my cousin Toni to see what she was doing, and to ask where everybody was.

"Toni, you saw grandmom?"

"No," she said.

"Have you heard from her?"

"Yeah."

I asked, "Is she okay?"

"Amber, grandmom passed away."

After I heard what she said, I broke down and cried. I swear, my heart skipped a beat. I didn't want to believe what I had just heard.

Julian Rivera

HERO OR VILLAIN

"I am from Chicago and I love music." This is how fourteen-year-old Julian Rivera sums himself up. With hopes of becoming a professional actor or music producer, Julian spends his days listening and dancing to music. He is also "a proud Christian and not ashamed of it."

Have you ever had your childhood hero become your life villain? Every single day, until I was thirteen, my father was my hero. We did almost everything together. Everywhere my father was, I was right behind him. He helped me with everything—homework, school projects, and any problems I was facing. We talked every morning. My father was not a drunk and did not drink every day, but he drank on the weekends. He also smoked every day. It was okay, though, because there were no signs of sickness for a long time. Now, my father is a fifty-year-old man, overweight, and medium height. He is a very smart man, but he thinks he knows anything and everything.

Do not get me wrong. My father isn't a bad man. He does not do drugs, kill people, or steal. He is a man who can hurt you or help you. In my case, it is in trying to help me that he hurts me. People say that words do not hurt. I would say they have not met my father.

He went to the doctor because he was having some pain and having trouble with his side. It was nothing big to him because he was used to going to the doctor and the hospital as a kid. My father went to the hospital for breaking bones, getting stitches, and other usual things. He also used to go to the hospital for getting jumped by people and when he got everyday diseases.

This time, it was not just a regular thing, not something easy to get rid of. We left the doctor and went back home, waiting to see what would happen. Late in the night, my father had the pain again so we took him to the hospital. I felt sorry for my mom because she had to get up very early in the morning to take my father to the hospital because she had to go to work. At the hospital, the doctors put my father in a room and ran some tests on him. While this was going on, my mother went to work and I went to school. When I got home, my mother was there and she took me to the hospital to see my father. When we got there, the doctor was in the room and they were talking. He brought us together and told us that my father had been diagnosed with kidney failure.

My life has been different ever since that day. Every day I have to go into the basement and get a box. I have to take it upstairs and have to watch my father hook himself up to a machine by a tube coming out of his stomach. Do you know what it is like to see someone not able to take a bath? He cannot play sports or swim in a pool. He can hardly walk, and when he does a lot of work, his feet swell up and he has to hook up to his box right when he gets home. He has to take almost ten pills a day. I know my father has it bad sometimes, but he takes his disability for granted. He is always swearing and talking about someone. He is always on my mom's back and is always dependant on her to do everything. My mother works five days a week from nine to five. She works downtown and is always on her feet. When she gets home, my mother either has to go to class or to do something for my church. She is always busy. Sometimes, I know, she would just like to sit down and relax, but that is always when my father wants my mom to do something. When my mother sends my father to do something, he gets mad and starts arguing with her.

My father loves me. I know that he does a lot of stuff to help me. On the other hand, my father puts me down a lot. He is always yelling at me or calling me something or other. I am a Christian, and I am a leader, so now I have to do a lot of stuff at my church and always have to be out of the house. My father does not like that. He is always on my back about being in the church. He talks badly about my church and it is really hard to listen to him. In some situations, when I would like to take the bus to go to church, he gets all scared and makes a whole speech before he starts yelling, which hurts my feelings. When my father hurts me, I try to brush it off and put a smile back on. But on the inside, I am not smiling.

My father had it hard growing up. His father was a man who would beat his sons. Because my father is the oldest, he had it the worst. He would get hit by his father like a man would hit another grown man. My father was forced to fight ever since he was six years old. He was one of those kids who earned good grades, but also earned respect. He went to school in Chicago, when the city was mostly Caucasian. He was first in his family to go to a Caucasian school, which was hard on him—so hard he could not even get As in gym because he was Latin. He made a promise to himself that he would never be a father like his father was.

I am finding my father's promise harder and harder to believe. I know he loves me, but when I mess up, he crashes on me hard. Almost every day, since I was thirteen, we have gotten into a verbal fight. He is trying to protect me, but it hurts me. Don't get me wrong, I love my father to death and would do anything for him. And I know he loves me. But, sometimes, I wonder—is he my hero or villain?

Ray Rivera

URBAN ARTIST

*Born in Puerto Rico, fifteen-year-old Ray Rivera is a die-hard football
fan, a music addict, and a burgeoning artist. Raised in a "graffiti-infested
neighborhood," Ray spent his formative years observing street art, taking in its
nuances, and ultimately letting it influence his drawing style.
College is definitely in Ray's future.*

I am an urban artist and the streets are my canvas. I was thirteen
when I started writing graffiti.

My life changed in eighth grade when I fought one of my friends,
Juan. He was tall, a little overweight, and had lots of facial hair. I'd had
problems with him since the beginning of the year, so I tried to avoid
him. He was part of a graffiti crew and I was from a rival crew. My graffiti
crew members are family to me and some actually *are* family. Crews are
friendlier than gangs. They don't do drugs, shootings, gangbanging, or
standing on corners.

Juan started throwing down my name, so then I would throw his
name down to get back at him. When you throw someone's name down,

you're dissing them—putting them down, challenging them, and saying that you're better than they are. Each person has an affiliate name, which is sort of like a nickname but also much more. It gets attached to you, it becomes who you are. It becomes *you*. When someone graffitis over your tag in a way that defames or goes against you, that marks you as a rival. That's one way that graffiti crews put down rival crews, calling them out and reclaiming territory lost.

It was war between me and Juan, and the streets were the battlefield and our canvas. A lot of graffiti artists tag and create art in Chicago. It is crowded with urban art on walls and buildings and trains. I learned how to tag and do graffiti by observing and studying neighborhood tag crew pieces. I would do my graffiti piece and Juan would try to claim the spot with his pieces. During our graffiti war, I had my tag on an "elephant," which is a small box truck like a postal truck. I tagged all over the truck after I got out of school one day. I had worked out a plan to get that truck for weeks. I had collected some cans and special metal-writing graffiti markers. I had spent weeks working on the truck while my fellow crew member and best friend watched out for me. I finished and my friend and I went home. The next day, I saw Juan's tag all over the same truck. He had written all over my tag. It was the last straw. After that situation, we both got really serious.

After having covered each other's pieces many times, Juan snapped after I did a piece over his. He approached me after school, at Carl Von Linne Elementary. Once he stepped up to me, all hell broke loose.

We were across the street from the school, on the sidewalk. No one was really there to break up the fight, so it went on for a while. It was like a boxing match with no gloves as we threw face shots and haymakers. Finally, the fight was broken up by some random guy. We both messed up each other's faces, but Juan left with his nose almost broken. I was angry at the guy for breaking up the fight, and with Juan for fighting about something that had been going on all year long.

After they separated us, a member from Juan's crew approached me and tried to fight me, but the fight never happened, because the same random guy broke it up. Juan and I got suspended from school. They found out because we were across the street from school and the security guard came out and told the principal.

That fight changed my life because I never talked to Juan again. My friends had to pick sides: they were either with Juan or with me. Some people I used to hang out with chose to be on Juan's side. Whenever I see those former friends, we just pass each other like we had never known each other—or worse, we fight with each other. It's a cycle of war between us and it's unending.

Karina Carrera

MY RAINBOW-COLORED LIFE

Quiet yet outgoing, fourteen-year-old Karina Carrera is a self-described germaphobe, which means that she's "very aware of germs." Her interests include Spanish music, math, art, and going to museums. When it comes to food, she's especially picky. When it comes to being around her family, she's especially funny. All in all, Karina is a very loving person.

I was on summer break. No school, no work. I was thirteen years old and my sister, Tania, was seventeen. Tania and I were both asleep in our room, and it should have been a perfect, relaxing morning. Then, I woke up in an instant; I didn't see my older sister in bed anymore, so I got up and went to the dining room to investigate. Tania was there, getting ready to leave for work at Children's Memorial Hospital. She told me my mom's stomach had started hurting, and that I'd have to keep an eye on her until my dad got home from work. When I went to my mom, I saw that her facial expression was calm. I guess she didn't want to worry me. It wasn't that long, though, before I realized the cause of her pain: she was going into labor.

I asked my mom what I should do if something went wrong. She was going into labor, *right there*! Still calm, she told me to just wait for Dad, that he would arrive at any moment. Tania left for work. Then, about fifteen to twenty minutes later, Dad got home. He arrived in a car he had borrowed from one of his friends. Mom told me it was time for me to wake up my little sister, Yazmine, and my little brother, Kevin. I obeyed. They had no idea what was going on.

My dad drove to my aunt's house to drop Kevin, Yazmine, and me off. It was normally only about thirty minutes away from home, but because of the traffic it was more like forty-five. It seemed like the trip took forever. My sister and brother and I got off the truck, and without warning, my mom opened her door and threw up on the ground. I was so worried—I thought she was going to pass out, or worse. The three of us kids walked to the door of my aunt's house. Before going inside, I looked back at my mom. She was red in the face from throwing up. It was a very hard sight to see. It felt like pieces of glass were tumbling around in my stomach.

There at my aunt's house, I didn't want to do anything. Kevin and Yazmine wanted to play with me. They played cars on a plastic mat with a picture of a little parking lot and a gas station. I yelled at them to leave me alone. I was scared, worried, and stressed. I wanted to know how my mom was doing. But Kevin and Yazmine kept on calling my name, wanting me to play with them. I was annoyed and wanted to be left alone, so I screamed at them some more. I was tired, so I leaned back in my aunt's living room on a dark blue-green plastic desk chair for a five-minute nap.

I woke up to the phone ringing at 1:43 p.m. The movie *The Land*

Before Time was showing on the TV. I heard my aunt saying on the phone, "Oh really! Is he okay? Is he the one crying?"

I knew then that Brian, my baby brother, had been born and that everything was okay. My heart was pounding as if I had run five miles. I was so happy that Brian had been born and my mom was okay. When I finally saw Brian, I thought someone had exchanged him with another baby, because he looked American—he was so white—rather than Hispanic. He was wearing a little hat and when I lifted it up, I saw that he had a whole head of black hair. Because of that, I knew he was Hispanic. I felt very excited to finally be with him.

A baby can change your life. Taking care of Brian helped me realize that I was a good babysitter, and will hopefully be a good mom someday. Thanks to this baby, I have learned how to love—not only as a sister loves a brother, but as a mother loves a son. I've learned how to be responsible and how to be patient with a baby.

Brian's hair has since changed from black and straight to honey-colored and curly. And, as cheesy as this may sound, my life has since changed from black-and-white to rainbow-colored. Before Brian, I would get up in the morning with nothing to do. All I did was argue with Kevin and Yazmine. Now I get up knowing that a little angel is awake already. When I peek in his room, I hear him playing with his toys, and I know he is just waiting for me to play with him. I spend as much time as possible with him. I don't know what I would do without Brian in my life, because he plays such a huge role in it.

As an older sister, I would like to teach Brian school things. I would also like to teach him about what is important in life: family, friendship, health, and love. As he grows up, I would also love to teach him about making good and bad decisions. I will also teach him about respecting elders, girls, and family members.

But right now, Brian is a cute one-year-old with curly hair. He can be a trouble-maker—he knows he is not supposed to open his drawer, but he still does it, and he messes up all of his clothes. He loves to splash when I give him a bath. He knows what he's doing and when I call his attention, he giggles in reply. Even though Brian is only one year old, he is very friendly, especially with me. His smiles light up the room he holds in my heart.

Magali Perez

MY MOM'S SECRET

Magali Perez is a very sweet and caring person; but if you provoke her, she just might stab you with a pen. She hopes to become a lawyer or a dentist in the future, but for now you can find this fourteen-year-old dancing at house parties and hanging out with her friends. Her hobbies include talking, dancing, shopping, and text messaging on her cell phone. She is an extremely hard worker and happens to be quite creative. She enjoyed writing her story for the 826 project, and she hopes it inspires you to write about your life growing up, too.

On a recent, quiet Friday evening, I was just outside of my house talking with my mom, when she decided she could not keep her secret anymore. She decided to tell my two brothers, three sisters, and me what had happened when I was in the womb. She told me that when she and my dad were coming to the United States from Mexico, there was this lady named Candelaria who was my mom's best friend. She literally got on her knees begging them to take her with them to the U.S. so she could baby-sit us while they were at work. My parents decided to bring her. Little did my mom know that Candelaria was a prostitute who had slept with every one of my dad's friends—and my dad. As soon as Candelaria got to the U.S., she got into an argument with my mom and my mom kicked her out of the house. We did not know about her for a long time, until my mom figured out that my dad was going out too much. When my mom found lady's underwear in his car, she concluded that my dad was cheating on her with Candelaria again. When my mom confronted her, however, she denied that she had ever been with my dad. Then my mom told her that she was not stupid and knew that she was with my dad. Mom fought with her because they were best friends, and best friends do not do that behind each other's backs. As time passed, my mom found a way to forgive my dad, but she never again trusted him alone.

My parents used to be such a happy couple. They were planning to get married and have a lot of kids, but they never got married in the end. When I first got home from the hospital, the day after being born, I probably felt happy to know that I had two loving parents and two loving sisters who would take care of me through hard times. They were the world to me, and I did not want anything bad to happen to them. When I got older and my parents would fight in front of me, I would break down and cry because I wanted to be a happy family, and happy families do not fight.

My mom remembers one time when she was nursing me and my dad came home drunk, wanting her to feed him. She told him to wait up, but he was not patient enough. He went to the living room and yelled at her, but she kept telling him to wait. Then he got very angry and pulled her into the kitchen; she dropped me on the floor without him even noticing. My two older sisters picked me up and took care of me until my dad left. After he left, my mom went to get me, but I was already sleeping, and she told my sisters that he probably did not care about me because maybe

Candelaria had already given him a baby. My heart broke when she told me that.

Fifteen years later, about five months ago, Candelaria came up with the story that she had been pregnant but did not know who the father was because she had slept with so many men, including my dad. She tested each one of the guys she had slept with, but none of them had fathered her baby. Currently there are only two men left to test: my dad and my dad's best friend. Right now I cannot stand to talk to my dad because what he did is unforgivable. My brothers and sisters told me that they do not know what they are going to do to him if he did father that baby. I do not even know what I will do to him, but one thing I will do is stop talking to him (and probably laugh in his face).

After hearing my mom tell me this long story, the only thing I could do was break down and cry; I just could not stand knowing that my dad had cheated on my mom when my mom was pregnant with me. I felt like running away. How could he be cheating on my mom when I was not even born? My mom was also crying. She decided to tell us this because my sister had just told my mom that Candelaria was going to bring her fifteen-year-old son over from Mexico to test my dad to see if he was the child's real father.

As of right now, my father does not live in our house. He moved out when I was about six years of age. My little brother and sister see him almost every day, but I do not talk to him or see him. I stopped talking to him about five months ago when I heard the news.

Waiting for the results makes me feel anxious. Will I have a half-brother? If I do, I would like to meet him. I am not mad at him—it is not his fault if he is my half-brother. I couldn't blame him for what his parents did. We will get the results in December. Until then, I will not talk to my dad or keep in contact with him. Part of me thinks he is the father, but part of me hopes he is not. If he is, he will have to pay child support for the past fifteen years.

This was the worst news I have ever heard. I cannot wait until he gets tested and the results come in because I need to know if I am going to have a father in my future or if am I just going to have a mother.

Armando Serrano

THE BEST COMBINATION OF SOUNDS

Fourteen-year-old Armando Serrano plans to become America's top celebrity magician. Hailing from Chicago, his talents include playing the guitar, fixing computers, drawing, and writing stories. He spends his free time playing video games.

I remember holding a guitar for the first time. Holding it in my hands, I felt like Eddie Van Halen at a sold-out show. Its colors were a unique combination of white, black, and brown. It was a generic version of the Fender Stratocaster. It had one volume control and one tone control. My favorite thing about it was the tremolo arm. The tremolo arm is a feature at the bottom of the strings on the right side of the guitar's body. It is used to bend the notes as you play them. Pressing down on the tremolo arm while a note is being played creates different types of sound. I would always use that tremolo arm to produce the best combination of sounds possible.

I got that guitar for Christmas. I had been asking for it for a very long time. I tore open the gift-wrap with excitement and ripped the guitar out of its box. It was about one o'clock on Christmas morning.

Six weeks later, I learned how to play my very first song. It was February 5, a Saturday, and my brother Joel's birthday. It was nighttime and we were kind of bored, so I asked my older sister's friend Robert to teach me a song. Robert used to be my sister's boyfriend. He had been playing guitar for a really long time. He made his own music and his brother was in a band. I knew he could teach me some things since I was just starting.

We went to the basement. There was more room down there, so the amplifier would have more space to be loud. Robert picked up the guitar and started to play "Master of Puppets." His hand was going up and down the neck like crazy. I was wowed, and wanted him to teach me right away. One part he played I picked up quickly. Other parts were difficult because they forced me to spread my fingers far apart on the guitar's neck. Since we had only one guitar at my house, Robert and I had to switch off playing the guitar while he taught me each part of the song. My dark basement, with its cold tile floor, created the perfect atmosphere for the mood of the Metallica song.

Before learning to play "Master of Puppets," I had never listened to much classic metal. I would usually listen to AC/DC, Van Halen, or Led Zeppelin, and probably some songs by Jimi Hendrix. After learning the Metallica song, though, I started listening to metal more often, especially Black Sabbath, Megadeth, and Metallica. "Master of Puppets" had some confusing and difficult parts, but I wanted to learn it so badly—the riffs, the chorus, the solo. After I mastered basic chords, I added some tremolo action to the song's intro and the solo. I struggled to spread my fingers up and down the guitar in some parts of the song.

That day in the basement, Robert stood over me, telling me which frets to place my fingers on. It was irritating because I was too excited to listen to what he was trying to say. I was still trying to master the first part of the song while he was trying to teach me another part. As I played, my hands trembled with excitement. I learned the entire song that day. It went from being a boring day to one of the best days ever. From then on, I knew that the guitar was meant for me. I bragged to everyone and showed off what Robert had taught me.

Now, I have a new Gibson guitar. It is solid black with fine yellow lining and a smooth rosewood neck. It makes me feel more professional. After three years of the old Fender Stratocaster, I got my brand new Gibson as a graduation gift from my grandparents. I think the Gibson is better than my previous guitar. Some of my favorite guitarists use Gibsons, like Slash and Jimmy Page. I still use my old guitar sometimes, but mostly, it sits all dusty in my room. I miss my old guitar and learning those first songs, but I have since moved on to a new guitar and new songs, like "Enter Sandman" by Metallica and "Betrayed" by Avenged Sevenfold.

My new practice space is the attic. The room is pretty much empty except for a computer, an Xbox, a TV, and some bed frames. Since there are not many objects up there, the amp echoes loudly. I love spending time practicing new songs and creating tunes of my own.

That first generic Fender Stratocaster changed my life. I found something new that I was good at. Today, I am no longer a beginner. I am the legendary guitarist Armando.

Ricardo Rodriguez

A NARROW ESCAPE

*Though easily distracted, fifteen-year-old Ricardo Rodriguez is capable of
talking on the phone for up to ten hours. He likes math, and enjoys taking
long walks around Chicago. He is proud of his two Spiderman-themed sweaters.
He draws much inspiration from his mother, who always perseveres
during hard times. Ricardo is also very proud of his hair—each morning
he puts in just the right amount of gel.*

I was at my house. Then I woke up in the hospital. I was all alone. I was
very scared. I tried to get out. I yanked out the needles. There were
five needles—two on the back of my right hand and one on my wrist and
another on my left hand. I got out of the bed and walked out. The doctors
saw me and pressed a buzzer and one screamed, "The patient is escaping!"
The guards came running and tackled me and dragged me into the room.
The doctors then put an injection in me so I could go back to sleep. After
I woke up, I saw my mom, Ana R., and the doctor. The doctor said I could
get out of the hospital that day, which I did; but I came back that same
night because I felt worse, and then I stayed for another week.

At first, the doctors could not find out what was wrong with me.

When they finally figured it out, they told me: I had salmonella poisoning. It was a deadly virus that was eating me from the inside. I was scared when they told me why I was in the hospital. They told me that if the virus was not treated I could die. I did not want to die. I was thinking that I was too young, that I had not lived my life. I was only fourteen years old. My mom stayed with me all the time after I tried to escape from the hospital.

A month and a half after I almost died, my brother tried to kill himself. My brother was twenty-five. He is Guatemalan and Salvadorian, with dark skin and long hair. Once, we were really close. He used to take me anywhere I wanted to go and buy me things. Then, after he got into a relationship, he changed with me. When they broke up, he tried to kill himself. I took it like it was my fault that the relationship failed because he started getting angry at me and he started hitting me. When I asked him for anything, he automatically would say "no." He drank casually before the relationship, but then after it, he started drinking heavily and chugging down beers.

I took all these changes hard. When he got back from the hospital, I started smoking weed and hanging out with this one crew. They are future members of this one gang. I used to chill with them and they used to give me whatever I wanted. Before, I always said to myself that I was never going to be in a crew. I knew that a crew could get me into trouble. It could take me to jail—it could get me killed. That is why I did not join a crew. But just hanging around with them got me into trouble with the police. One time, I had a sack of weed on me and I was high. I was alone and I was walking weird, so when they saw me, they told me to stop. I started running toward an alley and the cops followed me. I jumped about four or five fences. On the third one, I fell. I got a little scrape—I still have a scar. When I fell, I saw the cops jumping the fences but I got up and started jumping the fences again. I saw a doggy house and I jumped in there and the police passed by without seeing me. They went back to the car and started driving around the block for me. I was in the dog house for about thirty minutes. I was kind of scared. If I would have gotten caught, my mom would have found out and she would have been disgraced.

Weed did not help me in any way. It got me into trouble with school and with my mom. In school, I stopped doing all my work. Teachers would be talking to me and I would start spacing out. I used to be a really good student, but after I started smoking, I started getting Fs. With my mom, when she would tell me stuff, I would disrespect her and scream at her. If she told me to go take out the garbage, I would start arguing and just leave. I could not control myself when I was doing weed. I did not know what I was doing. But when I saw my mom crying secretly after we fought, I knew it was one of the reasons to stop doing drugs. I care about my mom a lot. I am her future. She says I will be the only one to take care of her when I'm older and what I know about her is that she will be there for me no matter what I say to her. That is why I respect her. I also stopped doing drugs because my brother is very important in my life and I did not want him to find out I was doing dumb stuff.

Right now, I have been drug-free for several months. I am a new person and I am happy all of the time. I do not get mad as fast as I used to. I cannot tell what would have happened if I did not stop what I was doing, but what I now know is that I am happy. There is no one who can make me go back to smoking again. I even helped my friend stop doing weed. I started talking to her because she was hooked on it. She is like a sister to me, so I did not want her to destroy her life. She started realizing that she felt better when she did not smoke weed. She now has been drug-free for a couple of months, too.

Weed does not help with anything. It makes everything worse. I thought I was happy, and almost destroyed myself. I thought my life was alright, but I was lost and confused.

Tiffany Mosquera

MY AIRPLANE MOMENTS

*"I'm the kind of person that doesn't like losing," fourteen-year-old Tiffany
Mosquera declares emphatically. Certainly "not the quitter-type," she
always tries to succeed. Her musical abilities are prolific and wide-ranging:
drums, piano, and guitar. She loves reading comics, has been to Japan,
and enjoys hanging out with her friends.*

E veryone's life is full of moments—little moments, big moments, and
unexpected moments. But even though many moments are special,
there are also those that make us forget the good times and wish we could
just go home already.

One spring day in 1997, I was ready to commence a journey I would
never forget. Where exactly was I going? At that point, I did not know. I
had a big suitcase, lots of clothes, and a plane ticket I could not read
because I was only four years old. I did not really know what was going
on when I arrived at O'Hare International Airport early in the morning.
After we boarded the plane, I felt excited to get to my unknown destina-
tion. I asked my mother, "Mom, how much more time?"

She answered, "Only sixteen more hours."

Now I wondered where I was going. I asked my mom, and she told me we were headed to the other side of the world: Japan. She told me we were going to Japan to visit our long-lost friends from Colombia, whom we had not seen or heard from in a long time. *Are you serious?* I thought to myself. I could not believe I would be on the plane for so long.

Can you believe it? Sixteen hours! There is not much to do in a plane for more than half a day. The only thing I could do was watch a movie I had already seen or sleep. I felt like I was on a deserted island full of rocks and tree trunks. Where would I sleep?

The floor of the plane was my only option. "Tough luck"—that was what my mom told me when I complained about sleeping on the floor or the uncomfortable chairs. There were empty seats in the back, so I put a blanket and pillow on the floor in front of the seats. My back hurt and the plane was bouncing.

My mom woke me up when the flight attendants started serving the food. This was the best part: the food. What a fiasco! It was some weird cold lasagna with some orange salad and green bread. I did not eat a single bite. All I ate for the whole trip was cran-apple juice and cookies.

We were thirsty after the long flight, so my mom bought a Coca-Cola, which she loves. But there was one problem: half a can of pop cost three dollars!

We were picked up by my mother's friends. As soon as I got in the car, I noticed things were different. "Hey, Mommy, the steering wheel is on the wrong side!" I said. The steering wheel in Japan is on the right side and, because there is a big time change, we had to stay awake all night to be able to sleep at night in Japan instead of during the day.

Even with such a rocky start, the trip turned out to be one of the most unusual and interesting times of my life. It was nice to see our family friends, and to be able to interact with another culture (my mom's friend is married to a Japanese man).

The plane ride back was much more pleasant because I was going home after a month and a half. The floor felt more comfortable, but I think I was just used to it by then. The food was better—I even ate all of it.

During my trip, I learned that not everything is the way we want it to be. Sometimes we have to get used to what we have and try to enjoy it the best we can.

Jessica Vasquez

THE UGLIEST DAY

Jessica Vasquez, a seventeen-year-old chicana, prefers to express herself through
writing, rather than verbally. And on the rare occasion that she is not
writing, Jessica spends her time listening to music, text messaging on her phone,
or partying on the weekends. A self-described sentimentalist, Jessica tries
to put on a strong face for her adoring audience. She is thankful to 826CHI
for allowing her the opportunity "to express something from
her past that completely changed her life."

At first, I had no idea Donna was my father's lover. Donna was married, and would always come to our house with her daughters and her husband. She had three daughters: The first was sixteen, a few months younger than me; the second was fourteen, five months older than my sister Daisy. The third, the "baby," was eight. Donna came over often, and as far back as I can remember. It was never strange, and she didn't come every weekend. My dad went to pick them up when she asked him to. Donna's husband never suspected anything. By the time he did, it was already too late.

I was five years old when I realized something was wrong. My mother worked in the mornings and my dad worked late at night. He would drive my mother to work, then go and bring Donna and her daughters to the house. Donna's daughters would sleep in my bed, and sometimes they would stay in the living room and play with our Barbie dolls or watch our TV. My mom knew that Donna would come to the house, but she didn't want my sister or me to find out. But even though she tried to keep it from us, it wasn't rare for me to see Donna come over. Sometimes I'd wake up and see my father with Donna on the bed. I would ask why was she there, and he would answer, "It's because she had a headache and decided to lie down."

Really, I didn't care that much. Donna acted politely to everyone, though she would always try to be extra nice to me. My sister Daisy was very young, so she didn't know exactly what was happening. I thought it would be better if she didn't find out.

But soon, my dad started taking Donna's and her daughters' sides when things went wrong around the house. Every time her daughters did something wrong, they would blame me. My dad was giving up his life with my mom for Donna and her children. After a while, it made me mad. When I saw everything changing for the worse, I started to hate them all—including my dad.

Before things started to change, I had an amazing relationship with my dad. Back then, he was my everything. I used to be an honor roll student at Bateman Elementary School. I was enrolled in many activities, and I was the best student in the whole school. I used to do the best I could just to make him proud.

We had been living in a new house for about a year when everything changed for me. It was a summer day, and I was in my house playing with

Donna's daughters. I had decided to go outside and play in the pool—the pool my dad had bought for Donna and her daughters. Of course, I had been asking for a pool for some time, but he never bought it for me. Whenever I would ask for something, he would tell me, "I'll buy it for you later. I don't have money right now." But if Donna or her daughters would ask for something, he would go to the store and buy whatever they asked for.

My mother knew about Donna and my dad. She says she didn't want to leave him, especially because of us. I think my mother didn't know that I knew too. She never made it obvious.

The day I caught my dad kissing Donna was the ugliest day for me. That was the day my world ended. All the promises my dad had made to me were suddenly broken. My admiration for him was gone. It was like a bottle being taken away from a baby. I came down the stairs and saw with my eyes that they were kissing. Donna saw me, stopped kissing, and slapped my dad. My dad said, "What did you do that for?"

I went running back up the stairs. My dad called my name. He said Donna had something of his and he was taking it back with his mouth. I told him, "Yeah, sure. Whatever you say." I asked him why his lips were red. He answered, "Because I was eating hot chips—that's why my lips are red." But I knew the truth. Donna always wears red lipstick.

I was so mad that he would lie to me. He knew that I had caught him, but he didn't want to admit it. Even now, he claims nothing happened that day. I felt really down because of what I had seen. I told my mom, and she started to cry. She hadn't wanted me to find out.

Things changed dramatically for me after that day. Since everything

I had done in school was for my dad, I just stopped doing my best for him. I stopped trying to do things right, and I stopped paying attention in school. I would cry in the middle of the class. Everything seemed meaningless to me. I had to go to summer school to pass eighth grade, and in high school I joined a crew. I skipped school all the time, spending my time drinking and getting high. It wasn't until years later that I was able to move on with my life, and to take my education seriously. My teachers never understood what had happened to me. They wondered why I would act like that, when I was an honor student, the best in the class.

It was seeing my dad kissing Donna that changed everything.

Nathaniel Alamo

COLORS

Fifteen-year-old Nathaniel Alamo enjoys these three things: money, football, and
his lady. He also enjoys playing with his bulldogs, Lucifer and Violet.
People used to consider him a bad kid, but his teacher considers him
to be the most improved student of all time.

I was six years old, living on Armitage and Kimball in Chicago with my dad, mom, five older sisters, and two older brothers. We lived on the first floor in a two-bedroom apartment. It was September of 1998, and I was starting first grade at Reilly Elementary School. Everyone in my home was gangbanging, including my parents. Gangbanging was a part of my life. Everyone except my aunts was a gangbanger. There was fighting, arguing, smoking, shooting, gang wars, and more, all going on right inside of my home.

I quickly became accustomed to that type of life. Even though my mom tried to protect me from gangbanging, I still asked questions and wanted to be a part of it. I was fascinated by the blood, killing, and drama of it all. Gangbanging was cool. By the time I was seven years old, my uncle was locked up on murder charges. He killed three gangbangers and even shot a cop who was shooting at him.

One Saturday morning, I was in my boy's backyard. Fat Boy was a gangbanger and a member of the neighborhood gang. He was sixteen years old. We were smoking in his backyard and I told him how much I wanted to be a member. He told me that it would only take five minutes to be "violated."

To join the gang, there is always violation. Usually you have to kill someone—but since I was just six, they beat me up instead. I was a first grader and proud to be the youngest member.

Fat Boy called up his boys, and they all came, except my brother—who was a member too—because he was with his girl and didn't know. Fat Boy took me into the garage with all of his boys. There were six of them, ages eighteen and nineteen. I was six. They told me to "ball up," and then they all rushed me. They kicked, elbowed, punched, kneed, and jumped on me for five minutes. After those five minutes, I was in it. I was bruised, cut, and bloody. They took me to the hospital. I had a broken wrist and ankle, and I was hospitalized for about two weeks.

When my parents arrived at the hospital, they yelled at Fat Boy and the others, but there was really nothing they could do. It was my choice to gangbang just like them and the rest of my family.

Before I started gangbanging I was a quiet kid who listened to my mom and went to church. I was a good person. Then I became mean, bad, and apathetic. I didn't care who I hurt. I drank, smoked, and gangbanged. At the age of six, "colors" became everything to me. If you weren't wearing a certain color, I thought I needed to fight you, and I fought a lot of non-gangbangers just because of the clothes they wore. When I was eight my chief gave me my gang name, "Little Mental Goonface," because I was a crazy eight-year-old.

Over the next six years I was in and out of school and juvenile detention centers. At eleven they locked me up for carrying a gun. I was planning on shooting someone, but I was caught before I could.

Since then, I have stayed low key, and I do what I have to do to stay in school. I want to go to college and become a cop. My mom and dad have stopped gangbanging too, and now my mom goes to church and she even stopped smoking and drinking. Before, I was a nice, quiet kid; and now I am the opposite of that. When other kids ask me about my life, I tell them not to be in gangs because it is bad.

Jamila Khan

DADDY'S LITTLE GIRL

*Fourteen-year-old Jamila Khan has many hobbies, including sports, dancing,
writing, art, photography, and interior design. One day she hopes to
be a photographer. Sofie, Jamila's sister, inspires her to live out her dreams.
Something you should also know about Jamila is that
she doesn't "let people walk all over" her.*

My dad and I were so close. He took me everywhere. Everyone told
me I was his favorite; it was kind of obvious. He used to take me
to his job, to the park, to the zoo. We did everything together. I loved it
when he made me lunch—mac 'n' cheese, rice, sandwiches. He bought me
everything I wanted and needed. I used to be able to talk to him about
anything—boys, school, *anything.* I was "Daddy's little girl."

That all changed the day my father called my mother and said he
had some good news: He wanted to introduce us to someone special. I
thought he was going to tell us that he was selling his house—my
home—and moving out of Chicago. His divorce with my mom had just
been finalized. I figured that, because he had a big, beautiful house and

no one to share it with, a move would give him a fresh start. When my mom told us he was going to introduce us all to someone, I thought it would be a family member visiting from Pakistan.

The next day—the day we now call "when evil came into our lives"— it was warm outside, the sun was shining, the birds were tweeting, and I was preparing to meet an uncle or aunt. My dad said he wanted my mother to come to hear the news. I was so happy to see my parents together in the same place. They were actually getting along, which surprised me but made me happy. We all went to the zoo together. There, we met Sofia. When I saw her I thought, *Wow, she is really tall.* My dad had told us that the person we were there to meet was an aunt—my dad's sister. We went everywhere that day, seeing every animal in the zoo.

When we got to the monkeys, I looked at my mom. She was talking to Sofia when she suddenly became angry. I didn't ask her why; we could always talk later, but I only got to hang out with my dad twice a week.

On our way home it was dead silent. When my siblings or I said anything, we were immediately told to be quiet. Things were tense, and I didn't know why. I was wondering what happened between my mom and Sofia, and I was feeling a little uneasy because of the McDonald's we had eaten earlier. My dad dropped us off at home. As soon as we were inside, my mom called us to the living room.

"Jamila, Shakila, Abdul," she told us, "I know you guys liked Sofia, but there's something you should know. She's not your aunt; she's your stepmother. Your father got remarried a few weeks ago." I didn't think my own father would keep this from us. It was pretty obvious he wasn't going to tell us.

I would have been sad if my dad had told us he was moving, but this was unbearable. My dad's new marriage meant nothing would ever happen between my mom and dad again. Every child wants her parents to be together, and I was no different. My parents getting back together had always been a dream of mine, but after this, that dream was shattered. Seeing my parents in the same place together made me think that maybe, just maybe, we could be a big, happy family again. But after this news, I knew it was not possible.

My mother told me, "The only reason I was with him that long was for you kids. I knew it made you happy."

"Then why couldn't you stay with him 'til the end?" I asked.

She said, "Because we weren't meant to be."

Every day after that, I cried myself to sleep. Every time I think about that day, I remember the pain, the sadness, and the anger. When my dad introduced us to Sofia, he told us Sofia was our aunt. At first I liked her, I'm not going to lie. But after my mom told me the truth, which my dad was too much of a coward to tell us himself, I was filled with anger. I wanted to run away and never come back. I felt betrayed. I felt like no one cared about what kind of effect it would have on us. I can't believe my father would lie to me like that. At first Sofia was nice, but then, like most "evil stepmothers," she started filling my dad's head with lies. Just the thought of my stepmother now makes me nauseous.

Now, everything is different. My father and I rarely talk; it's like we're strangers to each other. People always say, "Kids need a father figure." Well, in my case, I *do* need one. But unfortunately, I don't have one; and there's only one person I want as a father figure. I wish my dad and I could be the same as we used to be. I wish we could spend lots of time together. I wish we could make mac 'n' cheese together. I wish we could go to places like the zoo together. I wish we could talk about anything, or even nothing. But I know that, because of this event, we will never be like our old selves. I will never be "Daddy's little girl." I wish my dad would take the time to get to know me again. I really want a chance to get to know him.

Evette Murillo

CLASS OF '07

A Chicago native, fifteen-year-old Evette Murillo hates it when people interrupt
her while she is talking. Evette is inspired by her parents, and loves
listening to music, especially the Jonas Brothers. She eagerly awaits the
day when she will get her braces off.

The day of eighth-grade graduation was exciting, and at the same time, it made me nervous. I had waited such a long time for this day to come. I hadn't slept at all the day before; I could only think about the day ahead. As I got ready, putting on my cap and gown, I thought about how many people would be there. I was right. As soon as I got to the school I saw so many people. There were balloons, flowers, stuffed animals, and presents everywhere. It was a big day for all of us, and finally it had come. There were people all around and it was difficult to find my friends. I went inside the school where all the students were gathering, and when I finally saw them, I went running to my friends. They were excited, and everyone was ready to get started. We started lining up and got ready to go into the auditorium. From far away, I could see all the people that were inside, ready to see the graduates.

All the graduates went inside the big auditorium. As soon as I got inside I could hear people talking, and I saw kids and teachers. There were cameras flashing and both principals were on stage. On stage were two rows of chairs and there was a big blue ribbon above that said "CLASS OF '07." The curtain was long and red, and as I looked around I saw roses and daisies. The audience was sitting down and looking at the students, who were entering in two lines. My friends were smiling, but I could tell that, like me, they were nervous because there were so many people looking at us. As soon as I entered I saw my parents, sisters, and niece in the crowd. They were taking pictures of me and clapping. It gave me a good feeling.

That day was a special one for all of us, especially because we were only the second graduating class of Aspira Haugan Middle School. The best part of the entire ceremony was going up on stage when they called my name. I felt proud because I had worked so hard to get there.

When everything ended, I went to say goodbye to my friends. As I walked I could see that some friends were sad to leave, while others were happy. Everyone was taking pictures and saying goodbye. It was an exciting day, and a memory that will never be forgotten.

During graduation, I was very anxious and couldn't wait to graduate. After the ceremony was over, I thought about how important graduating and finishing school is, accomplishing your goals and then working hard toward what you want to be in life. I felt proud of myself. Graduating was an important step for me—it changed me and made me think differently about school. It made me look ahead and think about how graduating from high school will be another great feeling. Also, I noticed how much I had changed. Before graduation, I was a very shy, quiet person. I now speak more and express my opinion more.

My family felt proud. I was the last of my four siblings to graduate from eighth grade. I was on my way to high school and my future was limitless. I knew then that I wanted to become a doctor, and I am still headed toward this goal—among many others.

George Spataro

THE LETTER

*Born and raised in Chicago, fifteen-year-old George "Georgey Boi" Spataro
wants to become an actor when he grows up; he is certain that his intelligence,
humor, and changing eye color will land him a leading role. George loves
playing video games and hanging out with friends in his spare time, especially
Diamond, or "Sass." "There's nothing like our friendship," George says.*

I t's finally here! Thank god. Hope it's great news. I've been waiting for this
forever. Rip. *What? How? Why not?* As I read what I thought was
my acceptance letter to my new high school, I learned that I had not
been accepted.

My heart stopped. I wondered, why not and how come? I tried harder
than any of my classmates. I got four quarters of honor roll and did every
piece of homework. It was not fair.

There is a lot of pressure on kids to get into high school. The teachers
talk about the high schools, and representatives from the schools come
and talk to you, too. From the first time I learned of this school, it was my
first choice and I knew I wanted to go there. In the beginning of eighth

grade, you select your first couple of choices. Then you fill out applications from each high school that interests you. Finally, your parents sign them. I filled out eight different high school applications. My parents signed everything and I sent the letters and applications to the schools I wanted to go to. Once I finished, I could not wait to hear from the schools. I had six months of waiting. I thought about acceptance constantly, during school and at home. Six months later, I had gotten back seven of the eight letters. I had been accepted into most of the schools but was still waiting to hear from my number one choice. Then the bad news letter showed up at my house.

I did not know what to do with my disappointing letter. I didn't want to talk to anyone about it. After I told my friends and family, I felt better. Upon hearing the news, they were all upset at the school for not accepting someone smart like me. My family knew I was smart enough to do whatever I put my mind to. They thought it wasn't fair. The high school admission was based on a lottery and grades. It was one of the hardest to get into because you needed to score well on your state tests even to be accepted to the lottery. Without the lottery drawing, I might have gotten in on grades alone. I thought the admission shouldn't be based on luck but only on grades. Through the high school admissions process, I learned that working hard is not always enough to get what you really want or deserve. I wish it could be that way; I think the world would be a better place if it were.

I knew my family and friends would be supportive. I settled for going to my second choice. Once I got to my new high school, I was not as happy as I wanted to be and really didn't know anyone. I was not in any of my friends' classes and everything was going badly. I knew my life was going to have to change a lot. Now I realize I am in a great school. I think this is the best place for me right now: new opportunities and new friends. I think high school is going to be an adventure and I am ready to face it.

Enrique Colon

TRYING OUT FOR A DREAM

Fourteen-year-old Enrique Colon grew a beard at the age of twelve. Proud of this great feat, he is equally proud of his Puerto Rican heritage and his long arms. His favorite part of the 826CHI project was being able to write about basketball, his favorite sport. The ladies, he claims, admire his lustrous, curly hair.

Before joining the team, I never even thought about trying out for basketball, let alone being accepted. In sixth grade the security guard who worked at my school was the coach of the basketball team, and he told me to join because I was tall. But I was also fat and didn't know the first thing about basketball, except that you had to get the ball into the hoop and play defense. But I signed up anyway and went to the tryouts.

Before I was on the basketball team, I spent my spare time sitting around. I wouldn't talk to my friends. When I would get home, I would just turn on my computer, listen to music, and go eat in the kitchen. Sometimes I would invite my friends over so we could play my

PlayStation 2. My mom was barely home because she had to work at the dental office. That all changed when I joined the basketball team.

When I arrived at the gym there were about eighty people trying out. Only fifteen were going to be picked for two teams: the fifth and sixth grade team, and the seventh and eighth grade team. Well, day one of tryouts was hell. We had to run two miles, do fifteen up-downs, and two sets of suicides. Suicides are exercises where you have to run up and down the court from the lines back to the baseline. After those, the push-ups, and the sit-ups, I was tired like a hamster on a hamster wheel. When tryouts were over we all got into a circle, and coach told us who made it. As he said the names, my heart was beating and in my mind I was saying, "I'm not going to make it." The coach said, "And the last one for the fifth- and sixth-grade team is Enrique Colon." I was so surprised.

The first day of practice was harsh. We ran one mile and eight sets of suicides. We played scrimmage games against the seventh- and eighth-graders, and our coach preached to us abut boxing out the offense because they kept on getting rebounds after they missed the shot. Weeks went on, and we did the same things every time we went to practice.

The day came when it was our first game, and I was super nervous. In class that day I just daydreamed about the game. I could see myself taking people to the hole and making the basket and drawing the foul. When school was over, we all went to the gym to shoot around. I was thinking how tall and how good the players on the other team would be. It was minutes away from the game, and we came out onto the court with a theme song and everybody started cheering for us. We jogged around the gym once and then turned to half court and split into two lines for lay-ups. When the other team came in, we started laughing hysterically because the team was super small. Their center was the size of our point guard. We went to half court for the tip-off and shook the other team's hands. When the referee threw the ball in the air, I didn't even jump; I just tipped it back and the other kid had to jump and he still didn't get it. We beat the other team 32–4 that day.

The day of tryouts, I told my mom that I had made the basketball team. I told her, "We're going to the top, and we're going undefeated in our conference." Since then, I have never given up on my dreams to play basketball in college.

Stacey Watkins

LESSONS FROM DAD

*Stacey Watkins dresses to impress. The sixteen-year-old is a great dancer,
hairstylist, and friend. Her hobbies include smiling and making people
laugh. When life gets her down, she listens to music to lift her spirits. Stacey
warns people, however, that she's very talkative—though in the
end she is "a good person to all."*

My dad passed away when I was seven. In his final days, he would
sometimes forget who I was. Seeing him in the bed, dying, was
very hard for me. My sisters stood with me, and were there for me, even
though we don't all have the same dad. My two brothers were there, too,
helping my mom—she was having the hardest time. My grandma and
grandpa came over and prayed over my dad. They already knew he was
going to die. When I saw all of the doctors come into the room, I realized
that something was going wrong. My dad had been lying in the bed for
about three hours. Then, I guess he got tired of struggling. My mom told
my siblings and me that it was time to say goodbye. My father told me he

loved me, and to keep a smile on my face for him. Then we all left the room.

He was a very good dad to all of his kids. He gave us everything we wanted, especially me—he spoiled me. I learned so much from my dad. He taught me to never give up in life, even though there are bound to be hard days and sad days. My dad always told me that even though I might never be the best in anything, I would always be good at what I did. When he passed away, I think I took it the hardest; I was very young and I knew growing up without a dad would be very hard. Every child needs both a mom and a dad—there are things that only a mom can tell you, and things that only a dad can provide. Turning sixteen is a very important event for a girl, and not having your dad with you on that day leaves you feeling sad. Sometimes you need your dad to tell you something about boys, which is a very hard thing for a mom to talk about. Only a man really knows about boys. My dad would be able to tell me what a boy wants from me, but my mom can't. She just doesn't know. And only my dad would tell me what he thinks about the things I wear; my mom would just say that everything I wear is cute.

My dad was the type of person that loved to go shopping with his family, and to play with my mom. My dad was the type of man who never got mad at his kids when he was having problems.

Having a dad like mine has made me a better person. Because of him, I work harder in all that I do. My goal is to go to college and get a master's degree in education so I can work with little kids. I also think about becoming a doctor since all the women in my family are doctors or nurses.

When I look into the mirror, I see my dad. I see him in my eyes, my nose, my lips, the way I walk, and the way that I act around others. Even though I was young when he died, it feels like I was older because I remember what a good person he was.

In the long run, I want people to see that I have never given up. I owe this to my dad. He has made me the strong person that I am today.

Just as I have learned so much from my dad, I hope that other people will learn from my story: Don't take life for granted, because you never know when it's going to be your—or your loved one's—time to go.

Brandon Trinidad

MY AFTERLIFE

*Fourteen-year-old Brandon Trinidad draws much inspiration from Marianao,
"the best restaurant ever." An avid supporter of fine television programming—*
The Sopranos, *for instance—Brandon is also a comic book collector and reader.
His interests include rock music, especially classic rock. He is a decent
gamer who plays Xbox LIVE, and his goal is to become a video game creator.*

"Man, I hate this class, it's so boring," said Midget.

"Yeah, Big Bird has so many wrinkles she looks like one of those Shar-Pei dogs," I responded.

Midget and I were seated in the back of a dull room with cheesy posters on the walls that told students to "Be Yourself" and "Be the Best." Now the class was ruined by Big Bird. Our teacher was tall with a large pointy nose that looked like a beak with lots of extra skin on her face and arms. We joked around about both the teacher and some crappy late-night TV shows we had both seen the day before.

Then, suddenly, everything turned silent. There were no sounds besides heavy breathing. Everyone was talking, even my friend, but no sound was coming out. I knew something bad was happening. My small, boring class started to fade away from sight as the sounds of the class came and went. I thought to myself, *It must be my asthma.* Then my lungs closed up, the sound of the heavy breathing stopped, and so did everything else. I just died.

I was dead for just ten seconds, but it seemed longer. During that time, all I saw was white and an outline of some person. I heard my thoughts as I talked to myself in my head for what seemed to me like a few minutes.

When I woke up I was on a respirator. To the left of me were my family members in tears, their eyes like a sky during a rainstorm. I had died and was given the gift of life again. Two days after I got out of the emergency room, my family members were still shocked about what had happened and have been ever since. When I got home they treated me with such kindness, as if I was one of the most fragile things in their lives.

Because of this experience, I wonder about religion and the afterlife. I wonder about who that person I saw was, and if that really was my afterlife—or if it was actually my functions shutting down. I hope not to have an early death. I think about the white light and wonder who that person was and whether I was on my way to heaven or hell.

Now, I am more concerned and careful about my asthma and my diabetes, which I have since been diagnosed with. I take better care of myself. I carry an inhaler for my asthma and wear a pump for my diabetes. I am better prepared. My friends, family, and teachers ask me constantly about my health and well-being. Sometimes I get mad because I don't like to remember it.

Through this experience, I have become aware of how easily life can be taken away and how important it is to be careful and preventative, and to live every day like it is the last.

Mayra Gonzalez

DIFFERENT IN CERTAIN WAYS

Mayra Gonzalez is greatly influenced by her mother, who always encourages her
"to be a better person." But as this fifteen-year-old's life readily demonstrates,
being good and being crazy are not mutually exclusive attributes. Her
hobbies and interests include excitement, taking pictures of herself, and having
her own style. She writes songs in her spare time.

A couple months before my birthday, I started to wonder what it would be like to turn fifteen. I wondered if it would be the same, or if things would change; and if so, how? I wondered if I would think differently or do things differently, or if I would no longer want to do the things I used to do with my family and friends.

Now that I *am* fifteen, I do feel different in certain ways. My mom told me that becoming fifteen would be a big change in my life. I would start to look different, think differently, and act differently. My aunts, Carmen and Maria, were also looking forward to this because, as they said, it meant I had become a woman. I wasn't a little girl anymore— I was a young adult. For my mom, it meant the same thing. She couldn't believe I was fifteen.

Before the party, we had to go get my dress and the things we would need for the party. Preparation took two to three months. We had to plan everything, like where the party was going to be, and which food my mom was going to make.

When the day of the big party came, I was really nervous. We had so much to do, and I was afraid we were going to be late for church. I had a really pretty dress; it was pink, with lots of decoration on the top and bottom. It was a long dress, like the one Cinderella wore, and it came with a jacket which was really pretty, too, though it was heavy. My shoes were pink and had diamonds on them, as did the dress. At the party, my cousins were very happy, and so were my friends. They had a lot of fun dancing and playing around. We took pictures and had a really good time. My cousins made me feel special during every second.

My mom prepared the food. Everyone in our family loves my mom's food. They say she is the best cook ever. The food she prepared was Mexican. It was beef with rice and beans. Her food was very good, and even though it was a lot of food to prepare, she made it herself. The photographer came to the house and took a couple of pictures. Then we all left for church, which started at 3:00. It took us forty-five minutes to get there. Everyone had already arrived. Before getting to church, we had other things to do, like get the food ready and get dressed. I felt, in that moment, that it was the happiest day of my life. I felt really special in church, because everyone had their eyes on me. The church had been reserved for me and my family. It was a special ceremony. After church we went to take more pictures, and then we went to the hall where the party was. All my family was there, which made me happy because my family is from other places like Las Vegas and North Carolina.

My aunt's presence surprised me. Her present for me was to come to my party without my knowing. When we left to pick her up, I didn't know where we were going. My family told me we were going to the store, but instead we went to the airport to pick her up. I was really surprised and happy to see her again. She told me that I wasn't supposed to come to the airport, that she was supposed to surprise me when she got home.

I was sad that my dad was not with me in that moment. Since I've never seen my dad, my dream has always been to meet him and spend time with him and tell him everything that has happened in my life. I want to be able to tell him how much I need him, and what it has been like to not have him with me, and what I have always wished we could do together. If he were here, I would eat and talk with him about things, and just spend time with him. I would tell him how much I have missed him, and that I love him so much and wish he had never left.

Standing at the altar in church that day, I turned around to see my mom. She was so happy for me. My family was really happy and excited for me too. Since that moment, I have felt more grown up.

I am going to continue to change and grow up by learning from my mistakes. I hope to become a good woman with a good career and a nice apartment. I hope that I am able to accomplish my goals in life.

Edna Hernandez

ACCIDENTS HAPPEN

Her friends, family, and favorite teacher have been the sources of fifteen-year-old Edna Hernandez's inspiration. Outgoing, funny, friendly, and with a great sense of humor, Edna seems poised to take on the world. Her hobbies include reading magazines, playing soccer, and listening to music, especially the Jonas Brothers. However, be forewarned—her calm, innocuous appearance is easily derailed by chocolate or candy.

Everyone has embarrassing moments, and sometimes you learn from them. My moment happened when I was in fifth grade, in Mrs. K's class. She was a skinny old teacher with glasses that made her look vicious and sneaky. Mrs. K's had blonde hair and gave lots of homework, especially in science. That afternoon, my class was going down for lunch. My friends, Susanna and Deney, and I were all the way at the back of the line on our way to lunch. As we walked, Susanna was telling me about what she was going to be for Halloween. She asked me, "What are you going to dress up as?"

"As a witch," I told her. Behind me was one of the class pranksters, Max. He heard me talking to Susanna, but I ignored him. Max was skinny and sneaky. He had black hair, and loved to make fun of people. To me, Max was an annoying kid.

The next day was Halloween. Going upstairs to my classroom, I was talking with my cousins Francisco and Gustavo about whether they were going to go to a Halloween party. The stairs were big and wide and full of students in the hallway. I was so interested in the conversation that I didn't see a stair step and *BAM!* I fell. My friend Deney was behind me and we both wiped out. All the students looked straight at me. As I sprawled out on the stairs, I felt my face getting red. A kindergartner said my face looked like a hot tomato, and it was true.

I hurt my hand and my leg. It felt like a brick just came down from the ceiling, but eventually I got over the pain and my cousin helped me get up.

"Are you okay?" Gustavo asked.

"Yes, fine," I answered. But my ego wasn't okay. I realized that kids had seen what had happened. It made me feel so dumb that it felt like a pot of cold water had fallen all over me. My falling was going to be the subject of the day. I just wanted to go home and pretend it had never happened.

I had not seen Max when it happened, but he had seen my fall. On the way into class, he began to taunt me. I was walking into class and out of nowhere he came up to me and asked innocently, "What happened when you were coming up the stairs, Edna?" I knew he was going to shout it out and tell everyone. At that moment, Deney and Susanna interrupted him and told him to stop it. They were some of the kindest, most honest friends I have ever had. They began to tell one of Max's friends the story of when he fell in the bathroom, to keep Max from saying anything.

Finally, I realized that everyone has accidents in life. They might be embarrassing or shocking, but there's no way that we can prevent them from happening. Everyone has their silly and embarrassing days. By the time we were at lunch, no one remembered what had happened in the morning—the embarrassment I had gone through going up the stairs and my tomato face while lying down on the stairs. I got over it that day because my friends Deney and Susanna helped me and because they kept Max quiet.

One thing that I know about myself is that I am confident. Even falling down the stairs did not really stop me from being the confident person that I am. It was a lesson for me, and now for you, that accidents happen to everyone. You will get over it, and you will be laughing in the end.

Estrella Nieves

A MOTHER TO MAKE PIGTAILS

"I'm a young author." This is how fourteen-year-old Estrella Nieves describes herself. Interested primarily in poetry, she nevertheless hopes to publish her own story by the year 2020. She says that no one individual or event has been the source of her inspiration. Estrella is an only child who loves animals.

"Mom"—it's the nickname only my father can call me—"Do you want to see your mother?" I felt like all my emotions were striking at me like bullets. I felt pain, sadness, excitement, happiness, and extreme nervousness. I was only eight years old. "Yes, of course!" I answered. I didn't really think before I answered. My smile was so wide it seemed as though it could swallow my entire face.

I had dreamt for a long time about the day I would see my mother, but when I finally met her, my dreams didn't completely come true. I expected so much more, and I was truly disappointed. When I first met her, she wanted to talk to me; but I was only eight, what was I going to say? I had never seen her before, or at least I didn't remember her at all. I loved her, nothing could change that, but I didn't think we would be in each other's lives for long. I knew she was going to run away from me again. I felt like I was a disease, and she wanted to avoid me as much as she could.

When I entered my mother's small apartment, I saw her smoking at her dining room table. As I wandered into the room, my heart was pounding so hard I thought it was going to pop out and run away. She walked up to me about ten minutes after my father and I entered the room. She said hello and asked my age and how I had been. Fear, anger and sadness were all over my face. She talked to me as if I was a distant stranger who had walked into her apartment with a man that looked vaguely familiar.

As the day went on, all I could think of was how she was not the mother I had dreamt of for years. All I wanted was what every other girl wanted. I wanted a mother to make pigtails in my hair. I wanted her to brush my hair and tell me over and over that I was beautiful. I wanted her to tell me she loved me—and even though she could not take care of me, I wanted her to tell me that she wanted to. I wanted her to call me her daughter and not just by my name, "Estrella." I wanted her to tell me she cared about me.

Although my mother wasn't always there for me, she was still a respectful mother. By leaving me with my father, she gave me a better life than I would have had with her. Her only mistakes were leaving without warning or telling me goodbye and never keeping in contact with me throughout the last eight years.

Since that day, I have only seen my mom once. I did not want to see her again after meeting her for the first time. I loved living with my father. He did everything and anything for me. He showed me that he loved me, even though at times we did have differences. He even told me that I am the reason he is living and that I was a blessing to him. But that didn't seem to be enough. There was a part of me missing. For years I couldn't figure out why I felt so empty, and I found out it was because of my mother not being in my life.

I want people to know that they are not the only people that have been raised by only one parent, or no parents. I want people to see the severe emotional damage people go through when they feel abandoned. I want people to learn from common mistakes. I also want people to understand and see the reasoning behind actions or emotions. I learned all of these things when I met my mother for the first time.

I know I am an emotional wreck and she is part of the reason why. But in a way, she also taught me about life. She taught me that no one is perfect. Even if it hurts you must always do what is best for the ones you love. She also taught me that life is tough and that I should learn from people's mistakes. People come and go, and life doesn't always turn out the way you dreamt it would.

NO GUARANTEES

Estrella Nieves

They say people age by years
In reality,
We grow by memories
And age by life

There are two classes of human life
The fortunate and
The unfortunate
Luck is a game of chance

There are no certainties

As I learn,
Abandonment,
    disloyalty, and
        unhappiness
These emotions come without
Warning
So they say, expect the unexpected
The future is unclear
As life has no guarantees
Pain will always come free.

BROWN

Estrella Nieves

As our
hearts beat as one
Color means nothing
As I look around
Friends become family or
Friends become enemies
Who am I to lie

We are not perfect
As one
We are invisible

We are misunderstood
With our primitive ways

We buzz like bees in a garden
And our information travels
At lightening speed

Like a flash without warning

We are like a papier-mâché project
And our glue is our teacher
Without the glue we are only paper.

Anthony Mojica

A FUTURE GOAL

Fourteen-year-old Anthony Mojica was recently hit by a car, and would like to become a lawyer in the future. He enjoys playing soccer, and draws much inspiration from his father. Anthony has a pet parrot without a name. He wishes that he could wear his hoodie in school.

When I was five years old, I started playing on a soccer team called the Chivas. We played all the time and we always played nine against nine. We played many good teams. But we were the best, and we won all the time. Other teams beat us only two times. We played a lot when I was younger.

I like playing soccer because I'm good at it. I also like it because my dad likes it. He played when he was young; he was a goalie, too. A couple of times, he even coached our team. We talk about soccer a lot. When he gets a chance, he comes and plays with me and my friends. He's the one who taught me about being a goalie—how to jump and block shots. When the ball comes in, I jump to try to block it.

The first time my team won, I felt great. To celebrate our victory, we had a party at my house. My mom made tacos. Then the whole team went to the movies. My mom paid for everyone. We rode in my parents' cars. I can't remember what movie we saw. For the whole first season, we went to my house to celebrate every time we won. Now my mom works, so after we win, we go to my friend's house, or we have a party in my backyard. I like playing soccer with my friends because they will always arrive on time.

I still play as part of a league. I've been in the same league and on the same team since I was five. We practice every weekend, but I play every day. I play with my friends at Pulaski Park. We meet every Wednesday after school at about 4:00 p.m. My cousin comes to play, too. We play twenty games each season. This year we won fifteen and lost five.

I've been the goalie for my team since I was five. About ten other kids tried out to be the goalie, but I made it. We are still the best because I am the goalie. I am fifteen years old. I play other sports like football, but I still love soccer the most.

I have the same soccer ball from when I was five years old. My dad gave it to me. It is old and dirty, but it is still good and I play with it because it has special meaning to me. I want to play for a real team, like the Chicago Fire; I can be the goalie for them. That is what I want to be when I am grown up. Or else I want to be a football player for the Bears and be a linebacker for them.

Without soccer, my life would be boring. I might be on the street or getting into trouble. I've seen friends of mine become gangbangers. Sometimes I've felt pressure to join, but soccer helps to keep me away from trouble. Some of the kids I play with now had been involved with gangs before, but soccer has helped them stay off the streets.

Mercedes Vazquez

MARIA AND ME

"Music is my anti-drug," fourteen-year-old Mercedes Vazquez would like you to know. Born and raised in Chicago, Mercedes loves writing lyrics and poems. Spencer Chamberlain and her parents are her primary sources of inspiration. Her hobbies include swimming, drawing, meeting new friends, and shopping at Hot Topic, PacSun, or Zumiez. Though self-described as hyper, outgoing, crazy, and random, she cares about the well-being of her friends and family above all else. One day she hopes to work with technology.

Everything changes over time. Nothing is expected in life. You think that nothing can bring you down, until your life changes in five seconds or less. For me, that moment was when I found out a secret that everyone knew except my sister Maria and me. To find out someone in your family was really not whom you thought can really affect you.

I was just eleven years old. As always, I was having fun, running, and trying to scare the ducks in the park. On this particular day, my parents were with us. My parents had been divorced since I was three, so for me it was very weird to see them together. I remember that they didn't look very happy. Their faces looked as though they were breaking apart. Despite their long faces, I was playing around and felt like I was flying in the clouds. I thought nothing could bring me down, until that moment.

Two months before that day, it had been my uncle's birthday, and we had gone to California to visit our relatives. We arrived late, and when we got out of the plane, we saw a big group of people. About seven people whom I'd never seen before ran up and hugged me. I felt awkward. They started to call me by my sister's name, Maria. My sister Maria was fifteen or sixteen years old, she was five feet tall, and was neither skinny nor fat. She always smelled like Victoria's Secret perfume or shampoo. My mom greeted one of the ladies and told her that I was not Maria—I was Maria's sister. Then they focused on Maria, greeting her and giving her roses. I felt left out and weird. They made conversation with us and then my uncle's wife came along to take us to her home. We said our goodbyes and then left. We had good and bad moments that day, and for the rest of our time in California.

During the trip Maria started to feel weird around the new, unfamiliar group of people, with whom we were spending all of our time. I thought it was supposed to be a good vacation, but it was starting to become a surprising vacation. The new people showed my sister home videos of her taken when she was little, and pictures of her that my parents didn't even have. My sister started to wonder and ask many questions, like, "Why do they have so many things of me when I was little?" That is how everything started. All those questions led up to the disaster and surprise that I never expected to happen to me or to my family.

A couple weeks after we came back from California, my dad was sitting down with my mom in the park, when he called us to sit down too. As we did, my sister's face became mysterious, suspicious. When I saw that face, my smile began to break and I started crying and started to break down. I told them I wanted to know what was going on. My sister demanded to know the truth about her real family. I looked at her with a serious face, then turned and looked at my mom. My mom began to cry. It looked like a waterfall was coming out of her eyes. My dad's eyes looked like crystal balls. My dad touched my hand and held it really hard. When he did that, I thought my hand was about to break. I put my other hand on top of his and held onto him. My mom told my sister that my dad wasn't her true dad and the people we met in California were her family. My mom explained that she had had Maria with another man. He left my mom, Francisca, and Maria. Later on, my mom met my dad, Silverio. They got married and he adopted Maria, so she became his stepdaughter. Then I was born. As my sister got older, it was as though nothing had happened. But now, the truth was coming out. My eyes opened wide like an owl's and I just started to cry. I said, "All these years we were such a good family; now it has been ruined." I felt that the world had turned upside down. I didn't say much after that. I was quiet like a mouse.

My world—my life—changed in that moment. I knew I was no longer going to be that happy girl who everyone adored. I also felt that I wouldn't be able to treat my sister the same way I had. Before, we had always had arguments; but now I was afraid that it would be really hard for me to not say things that later I would regret, like: "Since you found out that you were adopted, you have all the credit and I don't. I feel like I'm the one that was adopted instead of you. I wish you had never come into my life." If I ever get mad at her, I could bring that horrible memory back into her life.

From this experience, I have realized that parents keep secrets away from their kids because they don't want to hurt them, but later in time the truth can come out and it can be harsh. When this happens, children will blame everything on their parents—but if this happens to you, try not to blame them, because they want the best for you. Even though it hurts a lot and it can affect your relationship with your family members, try to understand them too. They just want the best for you and they care about you so much.

Danel Lungu

SAMSON

Sixteen-year-old Danel Lungu likes playing with his dog. He also enjoys learning about foreign cultures and their histories — European cultures in particular. Audi and Volkswagen happen to be his favorite types of cars. His father is from Romania, and Danel hopes to go there someday. Danel is an avid fan of Criss Angel, Mythbusters, *and* The Simpsons.

I got Samson at a pet store. My mom and I were just there to buy some bird food for her parakeet. Samson caught my attention because he was the only dog that didn't bark. He looked sad. When I went over to him, he got happy, while all the other dogs barked at me. He was about eight inches tall and was sticking his paw out because he felt he needed someone to play with. I asked my mom if I could get a dog. She said, "Let me think about it." Ten minutes later, she said, "Only if you take care of him." I said, "Yes!" We took him home, and he was shy for a week while he adapted to my family and to me.

Five years later, he is now eighty pounds and as brave as a tiger. Samson is a boxer mixed with a Labrador and has stripes like a tiger. I decided to keep his name from his original owners because it fits his personality—strong and brave but with a reserved side.

I felt I had to be responsible in order to take care of Samson. I was only ten years old when I got him, and he was only three or four months old. I had to keep him healthy. Samson was a playful dog. I had to have a lot of energy to keep up with him. Sometimes he would whimper when he had to go to sleep, so I would let him into my room. During the day, we would go to the park, or I would take him around the neighborhood. One time I took him to the dog beach here in Chicago, along Lake Michigan. Samson was calm there. He didn't bark at any of the other dogs who were running around. It was sunny that day, so I took him into the water. We splashed around, and he shyly mirrored my actions. His paws, not used to the beach, enjoyed digging in the sand. We walked him around under the summer sun until he dried, before taking him home in the family van.

During the winters, he likes to jump around in the snow. I throw a squeaky ball across the yard and watch him retrieve it. Afterward, Samson is exhausted. He grabs his teddy-bear-shaped toy in his mouth, walks up the stairs, and falls asleep in the enclosed porch on the second floor.

We have a bond that has developed throughout these five years. I feel that every time I talk to him, he understands me. He never bites me or barks at me, only at strangers. He always tries to cheer me up when I'm sad. I take him for walks, and he is loyal to my family and to me.

Samson has changed me by making me more patient, more caring to animals, and more responsible. Every time I see him, he's calm. He's not in a rush, and he's always just sitting down and waiting for me to pet him.

He gets happy and wants me to rub his belly and then wags his tail which means he's happy. I have to take care of him in order for him to stay healthy, so I have learned responsibility. I help him stay healthy by feeding him, giving him water, taking him in for his shots, and giving him flea baths. Samson is like family to me. I have known him for six years, and he's almost like a person to me now.

Hernan Araque

MY THIRTEENTH BIRTHDAY

"I like to take pictures with my camera," says fourteen-year-old Hernan Araque.
As a devout Christian, Hernan likes going to church and hanging out
with friends. He also likes taking public transportation, messing around with
computers to see how he can improve them, making beats by hitting on
tables, playing basketball at night to improve his skills, and listening to music
for more than five hours a day. He hopes to become a music producer
or a professional basketball player some day.

When school let out, my dad was waiting outside in his car. It was snowing that day. As I climbed into the car, he told me "happy birthday" and gave me seventy dollars. It was my thirteenth birthday.

After I got out of his car, I started walking to my friend Roger's house. Roger had told me to get to his house before his mom left because she was going to take us to the mall, where I was planning to spend the seventy dollars on a shirt, a sweater, a CD, and some shoes. While I walked, I had my iPod Nano, a Christmas gift, in my pocket and headphones on my ears. I used my iPod Nano a lot; I would listen to it for hours.

Roger wasn't home. I had no choice but to head back home, alone.

While I was walking down the street, three guys in big jackets and jerseys were on the same side of the street, walking toward me. The short one was a light-skinned Hispanic with a black sweater and a skullcap. The average-height one was a brown-skinned Hispanic with a basketball jersey and a big jacket with a furry hood. He had braids. The tall one was a white-skinned Hispanic with a basketball jersey. He had a jacket similar to the average-height guy's and a fade haircut. I went to the other side of the street so I wouldn't be anywhere near them, but they crossed the street too. I started walking faster, trying to avoid them by running to the alley, but they started walking faster. I was really nervous. I wondered why they were walking the same direction I was walking. I wondered what they were going to do to me, or what they were going to say. My heartbeat rose faster and faster with every step. Before I knew it, they had trapped me in a triangle in the alley.

One of them, a guy who seemed to care only about money, came closer to me and asked if I was an A or a B [names changed]. I didn't say anything. The As and the Bs are rival gangs. The neighborhood I was walking in, where I live, is the As' area. The As protect their neighborhoods from the Bs. I had never seen these three guys around the neighborhood. The short guy, who seemed to be the leader, came up to me and asked how old I was, and I answered, thirteen. Then the third guy, who was big and tall, asked me if I had money. I lied and said I didn't, hoping they would just give up and walk away and not do anything to me. I feared that they would find my birthday money and my iPod as they searched me. The tall guy and the money guy backed me into the alley, while the leader was on the lookout for anyone walking by. The money guy picked me up and threw me against a garage, and the tall guy searched my pockets. They found my wallet and took the seventy dollars, and took the iPod, too. The money guy that was holding me threw me to the cement and ran away with the two other guys. My upper body was in pain. The back of my head hurt and I could feel a bump. I felt so sore and bruised as I walked down the street. I had just been robbed, and I was worried about what my mom and dad would say. I put my hoodie on and pulled the strings so no one would see me cry.

I cried my entire way home. I saw a police car by my house. I was relieved to see the police so I could tell them what had just happened. As I neared the police car, I saw that there was a guy in the backseat. Three guys had recently robbed him. I told the cops what had happened, and they said that they would call me back to the police car when they were ready to see me. They asked me to show them where the crime took place. I took them to the alley where I had been robbed. After I told them everything that had happened, they dropped me off at my house and said that they would contact me when they found something out. I had hoped that they would find the three guys and that the police would get my seventy dollars and my iPod Nano back. We never heard from them.

My mom and my dad were mad at me for losing my iPod and the seventy dollars. They said that I was stupid for carrying that much money in my pocket. They were mad and aggravated. They felt no pity. They told me that I had just lost my only birthday present and that I wouldn't get anything else. It was the worst day of my life.

The three guys taught me never to walk alone, and I learned that I should never carry that much money with me. There are people in the world who don't really care about you. The world isn't a safe place. As you grow older, the world you knew as a kid is gone, and you get to see what the world really is.

Maria Perez

A NEW HOME

Fourteen-year-old Maria Perez is widely regarded as a friendly person who "can make up to ten friends per minute." One of Maria's many friends was recently overheard saying, "Maria is so nice she brought me lunch." In her free time, Maria visits friends, goes shopping, watches movies, and takes naps.

The day you move away from the things and people you love, you feel so sad and lonely. When I found out that I was going to move into a new house, I was so depressed, and it hurt really badly. I was in the second grade.

I didn't want to move because I was so happy in the house we rented. We lived on the third floor, and my school was a few blocks away from my house. We had really nice neighbors who had become my friends. I didn't want to lose all my friends, my family and my school. I loved my teachers because they—Ms. Quiñoes, Mr. Rosean, Mrs. Carmona, and Ms. Ayala—were all so friendly toward me. I knew the principal as well as the office ladies. My mom used to work at the school, too—everyone knew me because of her. My cousins also went to the same school, so we used to gather together after school and play. I loved my school.

When my dad said we were moving, I felt desperate and I didn't want to go. He had bought a new house that was bigger and that we would own so we wouldn't have to rent anymore. I cried a lot because I didn't care if we owned a house or rented. My parents tried to convince me that moving away was a good idea, but I still resisted them. Every day I would cry or pretend we weren't moving.

Finally my parents gave me good news. They said that I wouldn't have to worry about school because I was going to finish second grade in my old school. I was so happy! I called my cousin Marisol and gave her the great news. She was so glad. I told her that I would get to go to her house every day after school. Then my dad would pick me up at her house. She said, "Wow, we are going to have fun!" Then she asked me if I was no longer moving. "I wish I wasn't," I answered, "but we are."

The following day, I went to school very happy. I told my friends and teachers the great news. They were glad I was going to finish the year at Reilly. I told them I would miss them, but I would try and come back someday and visit my old teachers and friends once I moved. Having the last two weeks of school to say my goodbyes helped me with the move because it wasn't so sudden and I had time to get used to the idea.

Now I know that things happen in one day but change in another. The experience of moving from my house and life that I loved so much helped me see that not all changes are bad. I love my new house too. I have my own bedroom and we have a backyard to use any time. The school I moved to was fine. I liked my teachers and made friends, and I could still visit my cousins. This year, I switched schools again—this time, to high school. I made more friends as soon as I started the year, and I have a few good teachers. Change isn't always bad. It has taught me many things, including learning that my parents were always right. A new house changed my life.

Jazmine Figueroa

GRANDMA'S LAST GOOD DEED

*Sixteen-year-old Jazmine Figueroa has curly hair and dark brown eyes, and she
prefers to work on her own—"Less distractions that way." When she is
not being entertained by her dog or fish, Jazmine spends her time reading good
books and joking around with her loved ones.*

It all started when I was fifteen. My two brothers and I were doing
homework, and my mom was cooking chicken and rice. My aunt
called, telling us that my grandma was in the hospital, and that she had
been diagnosed with cancer. She said Grandma's whole body was hurting,
and she couldn't move at all. While they talked, my aunt and uncle said
they thought she was going to get better, and my mom was hopeful. During dinner, my mom tried to talk about school, so we wouldn't have to
think about our grandma. Afterward, while my mom went to the hospital with my aunt, my brothers and I stayed home and watched TV and
thought about my grandma. She had had cancer for a month, and nobody
had told me and my brothers until tonight. I was upset.

My grandma was special, sweet, and kind. When I was young, and there was a homeless man on the street who needed money, she gave him her last dollar. She always helped the poor, even when she was poor herself. I always told her things about school, and even though she hardly spoke, she liked to listen. She loved everyone, no matter how things went for her family. She hated to be mad at people. She never fought with anyone.

Eventually, Grandma's health got worse. The doctors let her come home from the hospital, and told us not to give her anything to eat. The last time I saw her alive, she was sleeping in bed, dressed in a hospital gown. I couldn't bear to see her like that. Her straight gray hair was down. She was very skinny. She had to take pills. She couldn't get up. She had to use a bedpan. My cousin Ana had to help her take baths. She stayed in her room. My mom, my aunt, my uncle, and my grandpa and I stood around the bed, some talking to her and some talking about her. Everyone said goodbye. My grandma couldn't open her eyes, but she could hear us talking. She lived for two more weeks without food. Then she couldn't last any longer. She passed away, and it was very sad.

The next day we went to her funeral, and she looked so pretty. She was wearing a flowered dress. She had makeup on, and was smiling. She had fake doves around her, including one on top of the coffin. Everyone was crying. She was so special to us. Grandpa was especially sad because he loved her so much.

Then we had to go home. It was late. The next day, we went to the church. We prayed for her, and some people took her to the cemetery to put her to rest. There, we said our goodbyes. We put flowers on top of the coffin, and then they lowered her into the ground. The graveyard worker let us grab some dirt and throw it in the grave.

After leaving the cemetery, we went to Grandma's house. My older cousin Ana introduced me to the rest of the family—some of whom I had never met before, like my cousin William. When a group of us decided to play football in the backyard of my grandma's house, William played too. We had fun together. William is the same age as I am—sixteen. All of my other cousins are either younger than me or much older, and it felt good to meet a cousin my own age. He's tall, light-skinned, and Puerto Rican. He is smart. He plays all the sports, like me, and his favorite is football. He plays for his high school's team. He goes to school and does well. William and I were both close to our grandma, but we didn't talk about her. We didn't need to. When it was time for everyone to leave, we exchanged cell phone numbers. Later, we talked on the phone all day. I found out that he has three brothers, and that we both like football and basketball, as well as hip hop and rap.

Since then, William and I have kept in touch. We talk about what we do for fun and what we do with our families. I love having a family member my own age. When I have a problem, I can call him to talk about what is happening, and why I am sad or mad. I feel like I can trust him with my secrets. I haven't seen William since the funeral, because he lives far away; but we still talk on the phone once a week and message each other on MySpace, and he is planning to visit us for Christmas. I'm sad that my grandma passed away, but I'm also happy that I met William. My grandma brought us together. She would be happy to know that I met a cousin I had never known before because of her.

Amber Cintron

SACRIFICES

*A laid-back lover of body piercings, fourteen-year-old Amber Cintron enjoys
arts and crafts. Outgoing, giving, and with cool green eyes, Amber
loves watching movies like* Titanic. *And though she isn't a big fan of high school,
she nevertheless attends for her friends.*

I was allergic to cats, but made an exception for Pancho. I got him when
I was twelve years old. Pancho was tan with white paws. He loved to
play with toys that had catnip inside. I got him when he was four weeks
old, and he was too young to eat cat food so I used to feed him milk. I got
Pancho from Petland and he cost $329.54.

I remember the day he caught his first bird. I had just given him a
bath. He was always looking out the window, wanting to catch a bird, so
I let him go outside for a little while and he caught one. My mom and I
used to let him play outside, but this was the first time he had ever caught
a bird.

Later that afternoon, while Pancho was still outside, the lady who lived upstairs came knocking on my door. In a panicked voice, she told me two dogs next door were attacking my cat. Suddenly my heart dropped and I ran into the yard to see the guard dogs, Galaxy and Star, attacking Pancho. There was no grass in the backyard, only concrete, and Pancho was in the middle of it, completely surrounded. I was scared for my own life and I was scared to see Pancho. I felt helpless. My neighbor came outside to try and get her dogs off, but it was too late. Pancho was not moving, and I grabbed him and pulled him into my chest. My heart felt like it had stopped. I was so horrified I could not even talk. It was like losing a family member.

Pancho was two years and eight months old when he died. Thinking of Pancho still makes me sad sometimes. Every time I was bored or sad, he was always the one I went to for comfort. My neighbor started crying with me because she knew how it felt to lose a special pet. She felt so bad and apologized many times. Now, whenever I see other dogs besides my own, I do not automatically think they are nice.

Looking back, I wonder if I took too much time to get the dogs off of Pancho. In those moments, I realize that I could not have saved Pancho. I remember that, no matter what, we should never underestimate anyone—dogs, or even people—because they can turn on us any second. Before, Galaxy and Star were not that friendly, but they were still pretty nice. And similarly, in my life, many people have changed so suddenly it sometimes scares me the way those dogs scared me. Even so, we have to trust and make sacrifices in life, like the sacrifice I made for Pancho. If we don't, we will not know what it feels like to have something meaningful.

I am ready to trust again, and to make sacrifices in the future. I am getting a new cat.

Adam Tomazin

WALKING THROUGH THE HALLWAY

*"I collect magazines or books that I think will serve good purposes in the future,"
says fifteen-year-old Adam Tomazin. His hobbies include playing video games,
telling stories, listening to music, and preserving things so they will appreciate in
value. His friends and family are big influences in his crazy life.*

Walking through the hallway... along with countless teenagers...
glad to have my friends nearby. As we are directed to the lunchroom, my friends and I talk about mindless things that have nothing to
do with what we are doing. The hallways are narrow with red-orange
blocks in the walls. We get to the lunchroom, and even though it is much
bigger than any I have ever seen, it still does not have enough room for
the countless people. Whenever you try to walk, you always bump into
someone. My friends and I get split up. But being separated from my
friends means nothing to me now.

When I get to my assigned classroom, I don't see anyone I know. The
walls are plain with orange paint, and I figure that orange has something

to do with the school theme. I just fill in an empty seat at one of the tables. The teacher takes attendance, and I wait anxiously to hear my name. The classroom around me seems like there is something secret about it. People at my table talk, and I wait for an opening for me to start talking. One never comes. The teacher finishes calling names. But I never hear mine. She asks if anyone's name wasn't called and a few people raise their hands, including me. I'm not alone. The teacher calls the office, letting them know what's going on. Then we sit through an hour-and-a-half lecture.

When the principal comes to the door, I know it's about me. I think to myself, *How embarrassing it is to actually have to be taken out of class?*, and I bet the others are secretly making fun of me. They say I got the wrong schedule and send me to another classroom. The teacher in that class then tells me to sit with a lot of people. I lose my voice and cannot speak. This classroom is like the last, just not orange. Even trying to speak is actually out of the question for me. I just don't want to be embarrassed.

As I try to get my voice back I realize this is the worst school day I've ever had, and it doesn't get better. After lunch, I am on the second floor: I can't find the room with the right number.

The halls are dead silent, so I go back upstairs and search on the other side of the school. A woman there asks me rudely, "May I help you?"

I say, "I can't find room 216."

She looks at me as if I am some kind of moron. "It is on the other side, and this is the grade school side," she replies rudely again.

I don't even thank the woman because of how angry she has made me. I just walk away and find the classroom. This classroom is a reddish-brown; as I was searching for this room, I realized that all the classrooms on the first floor were orange.

Later, while I am looking for another class, some people walk by and say, "Got the wrong classroom again?" I just want to turn around and punch them, but I know I can't. I go to the next class, where I find two people that I can talk to. I am relieved and, for the first time all day, not worrying about finding the right classroom. I feel as though my entire soul has calmed down.

A few days pass, and I get so used to everything, but I'm still nervous to talk to new people. Then one day, I get home from school, and the phone rings: It is my ex-girlfriend. I start thinking about life before high school, and the life I left behind.

Ivonne and I first met when I was in seventh grade and she was in sixth. We were in the after-school program, where kids go after school if their parents can't pick them up.

One day, near the beginning of the year, a friend and I were messing with a *Mad Libs* book, where you fill in the blanks of a paragraph with any words that you want. At one part it asked for a name, and my friend replied, "Why don't you put *Ivonne?*"

"Who's *Ivonne?*" I asked.

Out of nowhere I heard, "Who's talking about me and what is it about?" I didn't say anything, but as soon as I turned and saw her, I thought to myself, *I would be the happiest person on this planet if she let me be her boyfriend.*

Throughout that year we became pretty good friends. We would always talk about our life experiences. At one point she even gave me a friendship bracelet.

The next school year I kept on seeing her in hallways and classrooms, and every time she saw me she looked like she was mad about something, so I never said anything to her. Then one day in late September, we were both altar servers at a Mass after school. When Mass was done, she came up to me and gave me a hug, but she wouldn't let go. At one point I said, "Stop, it's not like you like me," and then she said, "But I do."

I decided that I wanted to tell everyone in the school that we liked each other, and I knew I only had to tell one person to make this happen: my friend Gaston. I told him at lunch and, as planned, he spread it throughout the school like wild fire. Later Ivonne asked me why I had told him. I replied, "So everyone would know about us." I thought this might make her mad, but instead she seemed to like it—at least at first. From that day on, however, two of my friends were constantly making fun of Ivonne and me, and I am not good with comebacks or thinking of ways to get back at them. It wasn't only them, though. Everyone who even knew my name would make fun of me.

Then one day, out of nowhere, Ivonne said to me, "I think we have to break up."

I replied with, "You're kidding, right?" (I think everyone responds the same way in that situation.) She shook her head, so I walked away quickly and slammed a door into the wall, making a huge sound. I was so enraged because she had no reason to break up with me, and she didn't even try to come up with one.

We still talk on the phone. I say I don't want to get back together, but secretly I do. When I think about it, I realize it is kind of my fault that we broke up. I never really defended her or tried hard enough to do anything to make our relationship better.

When I got to high school, I was expecting to be treated worse than ever. I used to think public schools were worse than Catholic schools, but I've changed my mind. The students still joke and fool around, but not constantly like at my last school. I transferred out because I wanted to be part of the first graduating class at a newly opened public school. I thought that would make me memorable. At my old school people were always making fun of us, because of *us*. Now she still gets made fun of, but not because of me. I worry about her sometimes because we are not at the same school anymore, but she seems to be more mature when we talk on the phone. She's more direct about what was wrong with the relationship.

Walking through the hallway, here with my friends and sometimes without, I am now months from that first day and even further from grade school. I no longer bother to think, *How are they going to make fun of me today?* I think that I've matured, and I am not as concerned about what people say anymore. Talking to other people at school, I've heard their stories, and they're a lot like mine. Getting to know people makes you learn a lot about the world and yourself. It teaches you that you are not alone and sometimes everyone has felt the way you have.

Emanuel Rodriguez

HOMECOMING

"Every time I laugh, someone else starts laughing, too," fifteen-year-old Emanuel
"Manny" Rodriguez observes about himself. With visions of becoming a mechanic
or a car designer one day, Emanuel spends his free time plugging away at the
computer and playing video games. His favorite sports are soccer and basketball.

I t was a sunny day and I was playing cars with one of my cousins. I was
a little kid with light-brown hair, small for my age, and always wearing dirty clothes. I was six years old and living in Mexico in a small town
close to Toluca.

My cousin and I were playing in the dirt in our front yard with our
cars, and we were dirty, with mud all over us. When I went inside the
house, I saw my mom in the living room, standing close to the door. She
saw me all covered with mud, even though I had already changed and
taken a bath to go somewhere—where exactly, I did not know. My mom
had a weird expression, as if to say, "What have you done now?" She was
mad because it was time to leave and she had already bathed me. She

quickly gave me a bath again. When I was dressed and ready to go, my uncle was already waiting for us outside, sitting in the black pick-up truck that my grandpa had bought. I opened the side door, jumped in, and sat in the back row of the cabin.

I said hello to my uncle, and started playing around with him. Then my mom came in and told me to stop playing. She had a sad expression on her face. I didn't know why.

I sat down, and then my older sister came in, too. I didn't like her. She was short, dark-skinned, and ugly. As we drove away, and I looked out the window, I kept asking my mom where we were going. The look on her face said she didn't know what to tell me.

After a few hours of driving, we got to the airport. This was my first time at an airport, and I was surprised because I didn't know what I was doing there. The airport was big and airplanes were flying out of there. It didn't feel like we were waiting very long, because I was outside playing around with my uncle.

Suddenly, my mom said, "Look at your dad." I turned around and I saw some bald-headed dude that I didn't know. He was a stranger to me—it was the first time I had ever seen him. When my sister saw my dad she ran to him but I was just standing there doing nothing. In my mind I was wondering, *Who in the hell is that person?*

When he came close to me, he said, "Hi, son."

"Hi," I said, surprised.

They told me that my dad had gone to the United States when I was born so he could work and give us a better life. Now, six years later, he had returned to see us and take us to the United States.

While we walked to the car, he asked me what I had been doing in life and how my life was. I was happy and surprised – happy because I was finally seeing my dad, and surprised because I had not known I would be seeing him. That's how I met my dad for the first time.

After a few months of living with us, my dad got tired of living a poor life. My mom and dad decided that my dad should go back to the United States, and bring us there later. He earned enough money to do this in a period of two years, working without stopping. When he finally had enough money, he brought us to Chicago. Now that we're here we're having a nice life and we don't have to be poor any more. I was proud of my dad for doing this.

We have been in Chicago for eight years now, but I will be moving back to Mexico soon with my mother and sister. My father will stay in Chicago, to work and send money to us. I am sad about this, but my mother wants to be close to her family. I will go along and hope for the best.

Brandon Olivo

NO PAIN, NO GAIN

"I have no enemies." This is how the friendly fifteen-year-old Brandon Olivo
describes himself. Funny, goofy, kind, tall, and athletic, Brandon can
often be found playing NBA Live on Xbox 360 or surfing MySpace in his spare
time. And though his great love is playing basketball, he also enjoys
watching TV, listening to music, and doing his homework at the same time.
Despite his hectic schedule, Brandon is always there for his friends.

W hen I was in sixth grade I was lazy, tall, and fat. But one day, I
noticed that there were basketball tryouts at the gym. I knew
that it was a crazy idea to try out, but I also noticed that girls were
impressed with a boy who had skills in basketball. I also wanted to lose a
couple pounds while I was at it.

After school, I walked to the gym and I heard the ball bouncing
already. I opened the door of the gym, which creaked noisily, and I guess
that caught everyone's attention because they all stared at me like I was a
joke. The waxed floors were so clean and shiny, it looked like you could
eat off of them. As I had expected, there was a group of girls there, watching. The guys who were trying out were pretty talented and were in

better physical shape than I was. They were practicing for tryouts and shooting the ball at the rim that seemed ten feet high. I could smell sweat from the guys mixed with perfume from the group of girls. I went to the sidelines of the gym and began changing into my shorts and shoes. Some of the girls were looking my way, but I didn't know if they were checking me out or making fun of me. I heard the buzz of the twelve huge lights and the squeaky sound of the gym shoes rubbing against the waxed floors. I grabbed a ball from the rack and felt the bumps of the ball. When I had the ball in my hands, I felt a boost of energy. I started playing hard and began to sweat—a lot. When I'm in the gym I feel like I'm unstoppable. I feel very accomplished when the ball goes into the hoop.

After practicing, I felt tired and wanted to rest before the official tryouts began. I looked at how the girls were looking at the guys playing basketball and just put all the obstacles behind me. I just went for it. The coach called all the guys who were trying out to the middle of the gym. He said everyone had to stretch before we did the drills. I thought that the stretching part was going to be a piece of cake, but, like always, I was wrong. We had to do twenty-five jumping jacks, arm circles, ten push-ups, fifteen sit-ups and some exercise where you put your leg behind you while you're on the ground and lean on it. After all of that I was so tired I could have just passed out, and the tryouts and drills hadn't even begun yet.

I thought about all the girls watching and kept pushing hard. We had to do wind sprints and baseline foul shots, practice three-point shots, and practice our lay-ups for two hours. I was tired. My mouth was dry from no water. I had no saliva left. It felt like my heart was beating every millisecond. I was exhausted. But even through the exhaustion, I wanted to keep going. My teammates had complimented me on my skills, and I loved how that felt. Each time the coach looked my way, I straightened up from my exhausted pose and put a smile on my face. I wanted to make a good impression.

When practice was over, the coach called everybody to the middle of the gym and said that it was a good tryout and that the people who made it would be on a list in the office the next day. I crossed my fingers and hoped I would make the team. I went home so sore that I felt like a rusted tin man. I could not even walk the five blocks home. I had to call my mom to come and pick me up. I was hoping that I had made the team. The good thing about all of it was that I didn't give up in front of the girls, and I felt like I had lost a couple pounds. I got home, ate a sandwich, drank a liter of water in one gulp, took a cold shower, and went to bed.

The next day I got up and all of my muscles hurt. But I felt accomplished. I was living up to the motto of "No pain, no gain." I had tried my hardest, done everything I could, and felt good about it. I got dressed and went to school early and had to wait outside. I was talking with my friends, but I was not paying attention to the conversation. All I could think about was the list. My friends were trying to encourage me, as most of them were confident they would be on the team, but I was not as good of a player and lacked the confidence. When the bell rang and kids started going in, I ran to the main office and checked the list hoping to see the name "Brandon Olivo." When I saw my name I screamed a big "Whooooo!" while clapping my hands really loud. I felt like I had won the World Series or the Super Bowl. It felt like my day could never go wrong. My heart was beating quickly because I was so happy. I ran up to the gym and thanked the coach. He told me that I deserved it because even though I wasn't the best player, I still had enough heart not to give up and that's what the team needed.

The basketball gym is kind of like a second home to me now. Basketball has shown me that if you really try, you can do it, that you can accomplish anything you set your mind to. Basketball has also taught me discipline and timeliness. At first I thought it was a crazy idea to try out, but I was wrong. It turned out to be a very good idea—and it changed my life. Also, it made me healthier, because if you were late to practice, Coach made you run wind sprints or suicides for every minute you were late. It also taught me consequences and rewards of being a part of a team. We worked hard as a team to succeed. The lesson I share with you: If you work hard at something, you can achieve it.

Diamond Texas

KALEB

Fourteen-year-old Diamond Texas will allow you to call her "Sass."
She was raised in Huntsville, Alabama, and today she's a poet and a proud
resident of Chicago. When she grows up, she hopes to become an actress.
She loves to hang out with her best male friend George. Sass describes herself
as athletic, silly, and outgoing — and, of course, very sassy.

I had a moment, everyone does, a moment that woke me up from the fairy-tale I was living in. Death is a sad song that embraces even children. If I had known my cousin more, my heart would mourn.

My family always called me the crazy girl. All my life I lived by making jokes and acting silly. To be honest, it was like everything was a joke to me. And I always had people helping me with my problems. I could not have been luckier.

The birth of my cousin Kaleb was very special. He was my cousin Yvette's third child, and when he was born I was ready to care for him. Yvette practically raised me, so when Kaleb was born I was ready to return to him all the love his family had given to me. I babysat for Kaleb every chance I got. Even though he was little, he was a true blessing in my life. "My Little Joy," I called him. But now I understand, and I am sad to say, a wonderful thing had to come to an end.

On August 18, 2007, my Joy, my baby cousin, was taken from us. On the morning of August 18, we learned that Kaleb had died in his sleep. My mother called me on my cell phone. I was at Foot Locker when I got the call. I didn't feel anything at first because she didn't know for sure that he had died. My mom said, "I think Kaleb died." So we didn't know. Later, my aunt called and confirmed that Kaleb had died. He was only two months old. At first I was angry with God, and I demanded to know why He would do such a wicked thing. Kaleb was only two months old. How could He? But that was then.

After Kaleb died, I moved beyond my grief by living my life for his memory. But that wasn't going to bring him back. I needed to live my life for myself.

Death is a sad song, but the death of Kaleb has taught me a true lesson of life. One day everyone will pass. Kaleb's death taught me that life is short, very short. Nowadays, I speak up more and tell people how I feel; because things happen, life can end in a second, and I might not have a chance to speak up again. I just want to enjoy being a kid and whatever happens, let it happen. I'm not planning ahead.

I was never the type of person who "lived life to the fullest"—and that is not the message I'm trying to tell you. I'm not trying to tell you to do every crazy thing you could think of because you are not going to live forever. I'm saying respect life and yourself because life is short, too short. I learned this from Kaleb. I will never forget him, and I will never forget the lesson he taught me. If you want to accomplish something, don't hold back. You might not have a chance to do it again. Kaleb will never have the chance to live again, but the joy he brought to me lives forever.

Hector Miranda

THE PAPER WAR

*Fourteen-year-old Hector Miranda will laugh at almost anything, including
magic, football, rap music, and rock bands — all of which he enjoys. His hobbies
also include playing video games and watching TV. His inspiration stems
from his parents, who didn't have many of the things he has been blessed with.*

School had just begun, and a group of us started a war with rubber
bands and paper. It was one team against the other. By third period,
I decided to stop playing before I got in trouble or before something bad
happened. Fourth period and lunch went by with no problems.

Then came fifth period, and we were in Ms. Lockett's class. She was
presenting a slide show to the class, when all of a sudden a piece of paper
flew through the air at me. It hit me directly in the eye. The paper had
been launched at a very fast speed. My eye hurt so badly that a friend of
mine, Satchel, went with me to the bathroom to help me check it out. My
eyeball was so red. I thought this was mostly from my contacts, and I
took them out right away, since there was a big bump under my eye. I had

a lot of thoughts flowing through my head at that moment, and one particular thought was that I should never have played that game. I still didn't know who had hit me and I was eager to find out.

When I got out of the bathroom, Ms. Lockett started questioning me. She prodded, "Where did it come from?" I told her it came from the back window. She immediately knew who had hit me—a kid named Eric. Eric is known for throwing things, and he was sitting right next to the window. As it turned out, Eric had meant to hit Satchel. I went into the office to get an ice pack and to call my mom. She didn't answer. I told everyone I could stay the rest of the day. Eventually, Eric confessed to the teacher and principal, admitting that he had thrown the paper. He barely got into trouble.

I kept the ice pack on my eye for the whole day, and the bruise finally went away. The rest of the day was pretty normal. Getting hit in the eye didn't faze me at all, in the end. Even still, this experience taught me not to goof around in class.

Francisca S. Cruz

WELCOME HOME

*"I'm actually the best dancer in my dance group." This is how fifteen-year-old
Francisca Cruz describes her amazing talent. Born in New York but
raised in Chicago, Francisca loves to sing, write poetry, cook, and give advice
to her friends — when she isn't dancing, that is. She is also gifted
in her ability to "connect with people."*

The note said, "Clean the house." She had scribbled the note and left before we woke up. My older brother and older sister slept in the other room while I cleaned and organized the house so that when mom and I returned from the play, she would be pleased. Noel, my older brother, and Marisol, who we call M.J., would make the cake so we could celebrate when we got back later that night. I was excited: no school, my brother and sister were home, and it was my mom's birthday. I was thirteen years old then.

My mom and I had tickets to see *The Color Purple* that night and I had to meet her at the Sheraton Hotel on Rush and Ontario. It wasn't easy getting into the city from my house. I took the Fullerton bus to the red line train and rode the El into the loop. My excitement for the day turned to nervousness because I had a feeling that something stupid would happen with mom.

My mom drinks every day and has for the past eight years. She has a lot of stress in her life. When she is sober, she is a very smart, funny, and sociable person. I love being with her when she is sober because we have so much fun. She cooks for me or we go out to eat or to the movies. My favorite thing to do with my mom when she doesn't drink is rent movies and stay in the house. We buy all the candy and chips we can eat. It is such a big difference when my mom drinks. She gets mad about everything. You could try to be nice to her, but that would never work.

I got off at the Grand stop and walked a few blocks to the hotel. Mom was waiting for me and when I saw her, I could tell she had been drinking. We walked into the hotel bar where her friends were sitting. My mom is different when she is with friends, and when she is drinking with them she is hard to be around. They decided that we should go to a restaurant, and we walked to one by the theater.

The restaurant was different than the hotel bar, but that didn't matter. My mom was still having drinks and talking with her friends. I sat at a table, bored and angry. I wanted to skip the play and go home.

The time came for my mom and I to go, and we walked to the Cadillac Palace Theater. We got to the theater and found our seats, which were in the front row. I tilted my head back to admire the theater; the place was huge. My mom and I didn't talk before the play started. She was drunk and giving me attitude. I stared at the purple curtain and waited for the play to begin.

The play started, but it wasn't a relief from the behavior of my mom. She kept saying she wanted to leave, and finally we did. On the way to the bus she started yelling, first at me and then at a little girl. I was embarrassed. When we got home my brother and sister had not baked the cake. She was so mad that she kicked them out of the house. I tried my best to lift her spirits and offered to make the cake. I said we could make the cake together. She said she did not want me to and threw the TV on the ground and hit me. She took the phone and TV away, so I couldn't do anything. Then she walked into her room and went to sleep. I started to realize the effect my mom's behavior was having on our family. She was selfish. She didn't care about our feelings.

Two years later, my mom was still drinking. One night she came into my room while I was sleeping and told me I had to go live with my father in New York. She said she did not want me anymore. She called my dad and told him that she wanted me to go to New York that same night. I didn't want to go to New York. My mom was ignoring me and didn't want to hear anything about how I felt. I started crying because it hurt me to know my mom would treat me this way. I guess she was treating me this way because she had been drinking every day for ten years.

She ran out of the room, and that's when I heard her grab the phone and call my dad. I knew she was calling my dad because I know for a fact she wanted me to leave, and I heard his voice on the speakerphone. While she was on the phone, I tried to ask her why she was doing this to me, but she wouldn't even listen to what I had to say.

My dad said I could not move because of school. After the phone call, my mom went to the washroom, had a cigarette, and forgot about it.

I didn't forget about her threat to send me to New York. I was hurt and felt like I was nothing to her. I want my mom to stop drinking, go back to her old ways, and do family things. I want to have a family connection together. I want to feel welcome at my own house.

Susana Sotelo

SAVED BY A FRIEND

There are two things people often say about fifteen-year-old Susana Sotelo: she is
a drama queen and a great friend. About herself, Susana would say
that she is proud to be Mexican. Susana is also a dance team leader profoundly
influenced by music, and can sometimes be kind of silly.

I t all started one normal day in eighth grade. I was walking into the school building, and someone accidentally pushed me. I bumped into a girl. That girl, ghetto-dressed, was always getting into trouble. The teachers didn't like her. I tried to shrug it off, but I was scared of her. I knew she often made big problems out of small problems and had a short temper. She confronted me, and I apologized. She said it was okay. I assumed all was fine.

Later, I found out that she had told her friends and was upset about what had happened. My friends warned me that she intended to jump me. I was scared, but I told my friends that if she wanted to box, I would box.

After school, one of her friends threatened me. I decided to tell a teacher the whole story. The teacher told the principal, and they called her and both of our parents into the office. I was both scared and relieved. In the office, in front of everyone, she said, "I'm going to kill you for telling the teacher." Soon after, a restraining order was placed on her.

Three months later, we began to talk. I saw her on the street and she called my name. I approached her, and she said she was sorry. I apologized as well. She only threatened me because she was mad, she said. She never wanted it to happen. This time, I could tell that it was different because it looked like she meant it. We started hanging out outside of school in the neighborhood.

People began to accuse me of joining her gang. I always denied it, but because I constantly hung out with her, no one would believe me. I began to hang out with her guy friends as well. My best friend, Nayaly, became jealous. I could tell because she was always talking about how those people weren't good for me. She often reminded me that I was spending a lot of time with them instead of with her. She didn't approve of my new friends. She repeatedly tried to persuade me to stay away from them.

I was torn. The guys wanted more of my company, but I wanted to keep my friendship strong with Nayaly. I decided to stop hanging out with the guys and the girl because they were bad influences. Of course, they didn't understand. I started to distance myself from them. That summer, during a softball game, I saw the group. They wanted me to join them. Nayaly urged me not to go. I listened to her and continued to play softball. On my return home after the game, I saw the police. My heart dropped—there had been a drive-by shooting, and one of the guys was killed.

I realized just then: *It could have been me.* Looking back, I give Nayaly the credit. She may have saved my life. She is the one who helped me realize that gangs are not for me.

Anthony Gonzalez

TITANIUM BLADE'S JOURNEY
TO KOREA

"People know I'm unstoppable at martial arts." Fifteen-year-old Anthony
"Titanium Blade" Gonzalez does not mince words. Originally from
Massachusetts, his goal is to become a CIA agent, which is why he remains
disciplined and respectful in his daily life. His girlfriend, his parents, and his
friends are major sources of inspiration. His father once said to him, "If you
can't try, you can't fly." These words have remained with Anthony to this day.

The yin-yang is a symbol that represents duality in Chinese philoso-
phy, and a representation of how I approached life before and after
my trip to Korea.

There had been a lot of anger in my life. I lived with my mother. It
was a troubling relationship because we fought about everything. I was
misbehaving—at school, at home—and had trouble making friends. My
biggest problem was the physical abuse I had suffered from my mom's
first husband. He had tried to choke me, and my mom never believed me.
I was angry, so angry that I punched a hole in a wall. I wanted revenge on
my mom's first husband. I talked to my dad after and he said he would
take me to a special place. My dad took me to Korea.

It was the first time in my life that I was away from home for so long—two years. My mother thought I was going to France to attend school, but my dad had different plans. I would spend the next two years in Wushu training. Wushu is a martial art that focuses on the mind and rewards patience. It is about peace within. My father told me he had a lot of anger when he was my age and started Wushu. There is no place for those emotions in Wushu.

On the third day I met the top five Wushu masters: number one, Master Li of Beijing, China; number two, Master Akira (my father) of Nagasaki, Japan; number three, Master Yun-Fat of Taiwan; number four, Master Yagavich of Russia; and number five, Master Li of Korea. After that, the training got harder. They made me hold hot rocks under waterfalls, swim in rivers, and even spar against my masters. Korea turned out to be a spiritual and life-changing place for me.

While I was in Korea, I did not go to school; my teachers sent my homework through e-mail. One year passed, and I had learned so many techniques like Dragon Style, Serpent Style, Tiger Style, Eagle Style, Monkey Style, and Buddha's Palm. I also learned that revenge is not the answer. The anger I carried toward my mom's husband could be overcome with the peaceful practices of Wushu.

After the two years had passed, I prepared for the tournament that marked the end of my training. I was scared at first, but it turned out to be okay because my friends from around the world came to cheer me on: Ygor DeSousa, Ivan Manolo, and Takashi Kyoshi. I used everything my masters had taught me to beat my opponents. In the last match, it was me versus Tetsuo Akirayama, my cousin. We were both KO'd and so we went into overtime, when we had to break as many bricks as possible in two minutes. My cousin broke sixteen bricks and I broke twenty. I won the tournament thanks to faith, and got fifty thousand dollars, of which I saved part for college, and gave half to my mom, who is sick with breast cancer.

After two years in Korea, I returned to my mother's house. She had no idea I had been in Korea and still has no idea to this day. Ever since my stepfather abused me, I have wanted revenge on the world. Whenever I see my stepbrothers, I have anger built up inside and want to explode. I return to my room to meditate and they leave me alone. My mom has helped me realize that I need to leave the past behind and look toward the future. My life has had its hard times, but I try to stay in balance with all I learned in Korea.

I used to be yin. Now, I am yang.

Author's note: If you're wondering: Does my mother know now? Of course not, only my father does, so please don't tell my mom.

* * *

Editors' note: In the words of Barbara Grizzuti Harrison: "Fantasies are more than substitutes for unpleasant reality; they are also dress rehearsals, plans. All acts performed in the world begin in the imagination." Thank you, Titanium Blade, for inviting us to the dress rehearsal.

Karla Esquivel
BECAUSE OF CHRISTIAN

The only things Karla Esquivel—a fifteen-year-old vegetarian—eats are chips, soup, and cereal. Karla also enjoys hanging out with her friends and spending time with her little brother. In her spare time, Karla loves to dance and sing.

There was a time in my life when I didn't care about anything. I was twelve years old, and all I did was watch TV and worry about myself. I didn't leave my room for anything, not even to eat or anything like that. But I was younger then. I didn't know anything about life like I do now.

The day my mom had my baby brother Christian, I couldn't wait to see him. When I saw him for the first time, I couldn't even find him in the blanket in the car seat. My parents had just brought him home from the hospital, and he was only two days old. When they uncovered him, I wanted to carry him right away and protect him from the world around us. Christian changed my life. Now I'm like a mother to him.

He was the smallest baby that I had ever seen, and the cutest. And after he came home, I wouldn't leave him alone. I was with him all the time. I would carry him all the time. I would take him to my room and play with him. I would give him toys to play with, like teddy bears. His favorite was a little horse. I loved to make him smile by tickling him. My mom sometimes got mad because she said the baby wasn't going to want to stay in bed; he would want me to carry him all the time because he was used to being held. I didn't listen.

When he was three weeks old, I started to take care of him. I did everything that a mom does for her son—changed him, gave him a bath and fed him his bottle. During bath time I would be careful as I put him in the baby bathtub. I would even wake up with him in the middle of the night to feed him. I would take him from his crib in my mom's room and feed him. When I would go to school, time would pass slowly and all I could think about was getting back home to Christian. He had become like a son to me, and I would take care of him. I loved my baby brother and if something bad had ever happened to him I would have gotten mad—really mad.

At first he called me Jessi, my middle name. Then he started calling me "mommy." When I go places with him, people ask me if he is my son and sometimes I get mad because I think that I am too young to have a baby. One time at Kmart, I said, "Yes, he is my baby," just to see their reaction. They said, "He looks like you."

He is chubby with big cheeks and brown eyes. He loves to dance and play with his toys. He loves to take a shower. He loves to write and color. I love everything he does—like when he runs, he runs funny.

I love my baby brother, and I would give my life for him. I would kill for him and I'll do anything that he asks me to do. My mom tells me that I am going to be a good mother when I grow up. That means so much to me. She is very happy for me and I am too. I don't worry about anything as much as I worry about my brother. I don't watch a lot of TV any more. I don't care about anything as much as I care about him. It's all for him.

I want the best for him. I don't want him to be involved in gangs. I want a great future for me too. I would like to be a famous singer. And I want to have four kids, three boys and one girl. I'm a different person because of him, a much more caring person. He's more important than anything.

Yerazmin Romero

L.A. TO CHICAGO

Inspired by such divergent individuals as J. K. Rowling, Leonardo da Vinci,
and her parents, fourteen-year-old Yerazmin Romero treats
everyone with respect. Her hobbies include art, music, and literature as
means for self-expression.

I t was a hot day in Los Angeles. I was in seventh grade. I had fun in
school, especially since there were people there from all around the
world: China, India, Europe, Mexico, Ecuador, and South America. I had
a lot of friends that year. It was almost the end of the third quarter and it
had been a hard year. We had taken many tests and evaluations.

I was finishing my last class of the day. When the bell rang, I waited
for Aunt Angelica, my cousins, and my sister so we could walk home
together. I also waited for my best friends Julia and Petra. Our houses
were eleven blocks apart.

I was thirsty, tired, and hungry. It took forty-five minutes to get to
my house. Once we finally arrived, my aunt gave me a snack of jam with

egg and orange juice, and I started doing my homework.

When my dad got home from working at the refrigerator factory, he helped my sister with her homework. My mom got home from work soon, too. We finished our homework and went outside to play. Afterward, when we came back inside, we heard my dad on the phone with my uncle in Chicago. He took us out for dinner, and that was when he told us that we were moving to Chicago. L.A., he said, wasn't a good place for us.

When he told me, I became depressed. I didn't want to leave what I knew—my friends, my family, and my school. It was a comfortable place for me. But my dad said it wasn't good enough. He had never told us anything like that before.

In retrospect, though, I realize he was right, like always. There *were* some things in L.A. that weren't good for us, like the schools. My school in L.A. was kind of dangerous. It was huge, with lots of kids there, and people said that there were a lot of gangs. Teachers there couldn't pay attention to every student. On Cinco de Mayo there had been many fights in the school, though I stayed out of them. Another day, they had to close the school because there had been a big fight, and someone had been there with a gun.

One day in particular, I remember, I was standing in line on the playground preparing to take a test with our gym teacher, Ms. Taylor. While I was waiting for my turn, somebody fell and pushed the people around him, and they all fell. I was shoved too—my hip hit the wall, and I scraped my skin. I didn't notice anything until I went to my locker to change my uniform—when I looked, I saw it was kind of nasty. The skin was loose, and it was bleeding, and pus was coming out.

Since I was young, the situation didn't seem that bad to me at the time—but I just couldn't see it yet. At that time, everything was colored pink, and perfect. Everything was easy. As a child, everything felt secure. My parents had protected me and my siblings; I thought everyone was good, and that no one could make life bad for us. But my dad knew better, and he had seen enough.

The next day when I got to school, Julia was waiting for me at the entrance. She was sitting on a bench in the little garden in the center of the school. I sat with her and waited for Petra. The bell rang and we went to our first class: science. Petra came to school fifteen minutes late. I had planned to tell them both about what my dad had told me, but that same day, Petra told us that her father had left. She was really sad, so I decided not to tell them. My friend was having more trouble than me. A week later, I made up my mind to tell my friends. They were surprised. They got quiet. Petra started crying.

My dad decided that we would move at the end of the school year. I started to worry that everything would be more difficult in Chicago.

When I got here, my life changed completely—but mostly, for the better. For a while, I had a hard time in school, but my new life in Chicago was better than it had been in L.A. Of course, life here is hard too—but many people have it worse than we do.

Now that I have been here for a while, I can look back at my memories of L.A., and remember what living there taught me. For example, I learned that if we make mistakes, we don't have to complain about them—because thanks to those mistakes, we learn more about life. Similarly, this move has taught me an important lesson: I have learned that my family means everything to me. Within my family, I have everything I need—no matter where we are, L.A. or Chicago.

Raquel Gonzalez

COMING INTO FOCUS

"The thing I really like about my poems is that they come out of my heart and what I feel," says fifteen-year-old Raquel Gonzalez. Puerto Rican and Guatemalan, she takes pride in her honesty and her ability to be herself. Her hobbies include shopping, talking, playing basketball, and laughing a lot. She would like to dedicate this story to her mom and family, and the poem that follows, to her mom and Auntie Lilly.

F inally, I felt like I had done something right! Graduating from eighth grade made my mom so happy. There was a glow on her face. She was so proud.

When I was little I was diagnosed with ADD, which meant that I couldn't focus on my work like a normal student. It takes me a while to get focused, more than the average student, and I have trouble staying still, but she was happy that I overcame my ADD and got through grammar school.

When I got to high school it was the biggest achievement in my life, but also the biggest change. I met new friends there and I got along with everybody, but that became the problem: Friends! I couldn't focus on my schoolwork. I got caught up in who was mad at whom, who was going to get beat up, who was together or breaking up. Then my first report card came—straight Fs. My mom let it go without getting too mad, but I kept on getting into trouble with the dean of students, Mr. Ryan. I never wore my uniform, I never did my work, and I was tardy a lot. In total my tardies for that year were 165 and my absences were 135. When my semester grades came I had all Fs, but I didn't care. I had gone through the semester thinking I couldn't fail the year, but I was wrong.

Three weeks later they called me into the dean's office. I was crying on the floor. I couldn't stop crying. When I told my mom, she sat me down and pulled my hair and started to scream. She was so upset and disappointed. In the end she told me to try harder or she would take me out of that school. Since then she always stays on top of me and my grades. My mom sacrifices so much for my sister and me as a single mother, and the least I could do is pass this year. I want to make her proud.

* * *

I wrote the poem below about the drama in my life that happens inside and outside of school. I ended up failing my freshman year, and had to repeat it. When I first found that out, my mom was very disappointed in me. She screamed and made sure I understood how important good grades were. I never want to go through that again. Sometimes my mother will remind me of my failure to keep me focused. Thank God, I'm focused now.

UNTITLED
Raquel Gonzalez

Ashes to ashes,
Burns to burns.
I'm tired of
this and I can't
handle it no more.
Definitions to
terms of words.
I just want
to get out of
this world I
want to go to
the stars or
maybe the moon
but I know

this is important
something I need
to complete not
just for me but
for my mom
too. I failed once
I can't fail
again but hopefully
nothing gets in
my way like the
past or the future
I gotta step up
to the game and
so do you ...

April A. Thomas

LIFE GIVES SOMETHING BACK

Fifteen-year-old April Thomas is aggravated by oversized novelty pencils.
Growing up in various Chicago neighborhoods, April spends her time
reading poetry, dancing, listening to music, and laughing at people on the bus.
She looks up to her mother "because she's a great role model."

My mom started screaming and throwing up everywhere.

We had stayed at my sister Rachel's house the night before so we could make her a birthday breakfast and go on our annual birthday shopping trip. I had just woken up when I heard my mom calling my name from the bathroom. In between moments of throwing up, she yelled for me to bring her some towels. "Rachel, Rachel, hand me the phone!" she screamed. I called an ambulance. We were still trying to get dressed and clean the floor when the ambulance showed up. I told my sister I wanted to go with the ambulance. I could feel my heart pounding in my head the entire trip to the hospital. Once we arrived, they stuck me in the waiting room, alone with my thoughts. *What would I do if she died? Where would I go? How would I survive?* That was when I realized that I had been pacing back and forth.

My mom and I are like best friends. We go out to eat together, watch movies together, and we talk about everything. She is a mother of five children, three girls and two boys. She is a five-seven, caramel-skinned lady and she is nice to everyone. In fact, she is actually too nice. When my brother says, "Oh, I need new shoes," she'll buy him some instead of paying the bills. She's more of a quiet person. I get my writing skills from her. Some days she will sit in her room and write a play. We both like writing—just different types.

As I stood in that waiting room, I wasn't sure what to think, who to call, or what to do at that moment. I wondered: *If the doctor tells me my mom is gone, how would my life be?* When I saw the doctor walking toward me, my knees began to shake. I would have cried, but my eyes were all out of tears. The doctor told me my mom was going to be fine, but they would have to keep her for a week. After they let me into her room, I began to pray while she slept: "God, send me an angel."

My other sister came and took me home. In the car I explained to her what the doctor had told me: Mom was very sick from the cigarettes and had a huge blood clot that they were trying to bust without killing her. When I finally got home, I sat up in the dark, feeling very alone. I could never let her go. She made a happy home for us. I'd give everything for her. I told my brothers that Mom would not be home until next week, that she had gotten sick from the cigarettes and a blood clot in her leg would make her limp for a while. One of my brothers asked, "How long will she be in there and where is she?" I replied, "She's in Swedish Covenant Hospital for a week."

When my sister and I picked her up from the hospital, we were so happy to see her. She was limping a little bit, so we went to the store and got her everything she wanted. We bought her favorite ice cream, vanilla, and some apple pies. Then we took her home to see everyone else before we all went out to eat at Olive Garden.

Now that she's back it has been a little different. She'll stay at home a lot in her room sleeping or watching television. She's not as active as she was before.

This experience with my mom made me feel like I had no idea where I was or where I was going. I was facing a terrible disaster but then life gave me something back. It would be a mean world without my mom.

Armando Gonzalez

DESTINY DECIDES YOUR DAYS

*Fifteen-year-old Armando Gonzalez plays drums and soccer. He is also a
short-story writer and poet, who enjoys writing about love and life.
Funny, fickle, and sensitive are words he uses to describe himself. One day,
he rescued a cat—but that's another story.*

Have you ever felt like a complete outsider? Have you ever wanted
desperately to talk with someone—anyone—but people are treating you like crap? Well I have. It's not a good thing. It makes you wonder
all kinds of different things.

I had just arrived from Mexico, and it was my first day of school here
in Chicago.

It was 1999; I was going to be in second grade. I hoped everything
would go as I had planned: talking to people, making lots of friends, and
having the happiest first day of school. It was a beautiful Monday, a hot
day with lots of sunlight, wind, and a blue sky. I was in my room preparing for school: doing my hair, putting my clothes on. I was happy. I left

the house excited. I remember looking back at the house, and it felt as though the house didn't want me to go.

I turned away and was ready for school.

As my mom drove me to school, I wondered: *Will the teacher like me? Would I make a lot of friends? Would I be popular enough to make all the friends I wanted?* I stopped thinking for a second, leaving all my worried thoughts behind and hoping for the best. Finally, the car stopped. The school looked as big as the Sears Tower. I stepped out of the car and started walking to the front door. I went in, ready to face my destiny. I looked back at my mom and I could see she was nervous. So was I. The principal, Mr. Gilion, came and took me to my classroom. He was tall with long hair. I was excited because I had never been to a Chicago school before.

I went into the classroom and my principal presented me to the class. My teacher, Ms. Alvarado, said, "Hi." I remember she was wearing a long Mexican dress and big boots. She told me to go to my seat, so I did. I felt very nervous. It was as though a dead person had entered the room and everyone was staring at him, at me. I was there in my chair alone. I tried to make conversation, but every time I did the others would ignore me, as if no one was there. I was sad. Suddenly, Ms. Alvarado told me to go up to the board and do a math problem. I did it, but everyone was laughing at me. I took a look back at the board and realized I had made a big mistake. I felt like dying and wished I had never been born. It was the most embarrassing moment of my life.

Finally, it was lunch period. I wanted to sit at a table with other students, but no one wanted me, so instead I sat alone with only myself to talk to. I put my head down and started crying.

After lunch the teacher picked us up and took us to gym. Our gym teacher, Mr. Vega, said we were going to play soccer. I realized that this could be my way in, because I knew I was good at soccer. While we were playing, two kids came up to me and said, "You ain't no good. You suck. You don't know how to play soccer." I looked down and continued playing, but it was like the words they were saying were killing me.

Back in the classroom, I looked at the clock. It was almost time to go, with only fifteen minutes remaining. I was desperate to leave and never come back. I was at my desk, alone, when out of nowhere a girl came up to me. I hadn't noticed her before, but she was in my class. I started talking with her, and I quickly realized how much we had in common. She told me that she didn't like what was happening to the rain forest—killing trees to make houses—and I felt the exact same way. She made my last fifteen minutes the happiest of the day. It was time to go. We waved goodbye to each other and left. When my mom asked how my first day went, I told her simply, "Not bad."

It had been a long first day. I went to school thinking that everything would go just as I had planned. I was wrong. It didn't happen the way I wanted, but in the end, my sad day turned into a happy day. Some things just can't happen the way you want. In fact, destiny is the one who decides your days.

Karrie Chatman

GREAT-GRANDMA ANNIE MACABEE

*Karrie Chatman's family is not a big one, but it sure seems like it sometimes.
Fourteen-year-old Karrie lives in Chicago with her mom and dad, and
she has three older siblings. She has always loved writing stories, but until now
has never completed them and shown them to the world. During her
spare time she enjoys hanging out with friends, going to the mall, watching
movies, and traveling. Her travels to Europe, in particular, have
profoundly changed her outlook on life. Self-described as loving, caring, flirty,
and fun, Karrie firmly believes anything is possible.*

A s I sit down in the seat, I look around. I see things that make me
sad. I see people crying and people dressed in black making the
room look darker than it really is. Everybody's face looks lost, like they
don't know where to go from here or there. These people are confused.
They don't understand why God took her. They can't figure out why God
couldn't improve her health. They wonder where she may live in her afterlife. They aren't sure whether the walls of hell will close in on her or the
golden gates of heaven will open and comfort her. They are starting to
realize that her physical self is gone, but her soul remains alive forever.

Seeing these expressions on people's faces makes me think—should
I be sad too? Because I don't look sad. I look happy, like she's not even

gone. Why should I be happy that she's gone and everyone else thinks the opposite? Now I am confused.

I think to myself about how my Great-Grandma Annie MacAbee was such a creative, loving, caring, and fantastic person. Her creativity brought life to us when we were feeling stone cold dead. It made us feel like life was worth enjoying. She always came up with unique ways to keep our adventurous minds going and going. She was loving to all who wanted or needed love because she wanted to be. Her love supported and lifted us through hard times. She cared for us, and that was why we loved her. She told me that she lived to care for people. This made her fantastic in so many ways. And these are just a few of the things about her that explain how wonderful she was.

So now, at her funeral, I'm thinking of all the things that made my grandma who she was, and I can't find one reason to be sad or upset or to feel anguish.

Now it is time to go look at the body in the casket. My sister asks me if I want to go see her, but I say no. I think, *I'd rather have an image of her alive than dead.* So my sister Tiffany goes to see her by herself. As people pass the casket, they cry more, while grabbing her, hugging her, saying things like, "Why, God, why did you take her away?!" All I do is look around the church. I can't believe I am looking so blankly into space. Finally, I snap out of it and a beautiful singing voice is ringing in my ear. The funeral is over. My family goes to the cemetery. We put flowers on the casket. Then, we go home to eat and to reminisce about all the good things she had accomplished in life and all the greatness she had bestowed upon us because she loved us.

* * *

A few months after the funeral, I was at home and trying to go to sleep.

"Ma! Maaaa!" I screamed.

"Yes, Karrie, what is it?" she asked.

"I can't do it, Ma. I can't go to sleep. What if I don't wake up? What if I die in my sleep? I don't want to die. I want to live."

"Karrie, you have to stop talking like this," she said with great worry in her voice. "You are not going to die," she explained.

"You don't know that, Ma. What if, Ma, what if?" I cried so much you would have thought my tears were a waterfall. This had been happening for at least a couple of days now. Here I was thinking I was going to die if I slept for even five minutes. I couldn't believe I was thinking these thoughts. The devil was in me for sure this time and he wouldn't leave me alone.

As time went on, things got worse. I got to the point where I thought I didn't deserve to live. All I remember was me with a knife in my hand thinking to myself, "Do it, do it, Karrie," but I didn't because I didn't want to. I began to cry because the devil was taking over my beautiful mind that God had created.

Life was not fun for me anymore. The movies were not funny to me. My family and friends were not making me happy anymore. School was not even making me a little happy, though I never really liked school. Nothing was changing for the better, only for the worse. I could not stand it anymore. I needed to do something, but I did not know what.

One day, my mom called me and told me to get dressed because she wanted to take me somewhere. I got ready and she called again, this time to tell me she and my dad were waiting outside. I ran to the car, kissed my mom, and got in. As we drove, we talked.

"Karrie," my mom said with a sigh, "I want you to get some help with your feelings. I love you very much and I want to make sure you do not hurt yourself with your thoughts. So I am taking you to therapy. I think this will help you in the long run. Are you alright with that?"

"Yeah, Ma, I am alright with that," I said back.

My dad didn't say anything the whole time on the car ride. It was strange, but I guess he was thinking. I still wonder what he was thinking.

We arrived at the hospital and we walked to this certain section where they held therapy classes. We got onto the elevator and went to the third floor. As we walked through the place, I saw a lot of kids. And I started to think to myself, *I'm not alone. There are a lot of other kids with problems like mine.* My therapy teacher came and got me and took me into her office. She asked a lot of questions about my feelings, my life, my family, and other important issues. I asked her when I would start the class. "Oh, not today," she said. "I'm just asking questions so I can get to know you better." "Okay," I said, sounding confused. Afterward, we left and got some take-out. We went home and ate the food while watching a movie. I felt encouraged about the class, because it might help me figure out my problems.

I had been going to therapy for a few weeks, and, honestly, it was not working. My attitude was getting worse. I was making the wrong kinds of friends. I was talking back to my parents. I was having temper tantrums all over the place. My life had really fallen downhill. Eventually, my mom started to think therapy wasn't working and she decided to take me out of it. I didn't go to therapy anymore and I was quite fine with it. School had started already, and it was keeping me occupied from evil thoughts that still came to my mind at night. Life was going okay from then on.

It has been a few years since all of this happened. I'm doing a lot better in the "thought" department. As for my attitude, well, that's another story. I'm currently attending Aspira Early College High School as a young freshman. My friends are cool, and they've got my back like I've got theirs. So I'm doing a lot better—but when my great-grandma's birthday comes around, I say, "Happy Birthday, Grandma," and I still get sad, but I know my Grandma's got my back with love and support for me.

Angelica Troche

TRIAL BY FIRE

"I am said to be 'wise beyond my years,'" fourteen-year-old Angelica Troche
would like you to know. Quiet with strangers and wild with friends,
Angelica loves to dance and write poetry. She is honest, smart, and down-
to-earth. Her family and friends inspire her. She hopes to inspire you.

It was one apartment. So many memories attached to just one apartment. A different memory attached to each room, each area. That night, when we arrived at the corner of our block, everything was smoky. Things seemed so far away—even things that were right in front of us. Our block was crowded with fire trucks and ambulances and police cars. My grandpa, after picking up my two cousins from the South Side, let us out at Laramie and Roscoe and told us to call him, to let him know everything was okay. It was late evening. I could hear people talking, but I could not make out what they were saying over the loud beating of my heart. It was almost winter. The cold was not helping; I was worried, anxious, and scared. I could feel the butterflies in my stomach going crazy.

My mom, my cousins Mikey and Julie, and my baby brother stood next to me. Still, I felt so alone. The closer we got, the more intense the feelings that something was wrong became, and the more the butterflies fluttered. I hadn't heard from my dad in a while, but my mom was there with my brother. When we got closer, our neighbors from a couple doors down recognized us immediately and came up to us right away.

We stopped. Mikey and Julie, neither of them ten years old yet, dropped the bags they were carrying and began to talk to me, to comfort me. I was only a fifth-grader. My heart was going a thousand beats per minute. I felt so upset. My home was on fire. I knew I still had to face the facts. It was all gone, demolished, marred—nothing could have changed it. That was a fact.

No one unprotected was allowed into the building. They told us the fire had been put out a couple minutes before we arrived. They also told us that a firefighter had been injured; he had fallen through the floor in the kitchen and broken his jaw. I felt bad for him, but had more sympathy for myself. My brother, my cousins, and I went to the neighbors' house while my mom talked to police officers and firefighters. They told my mom it all started in the back bedroom, on the first floor—right below my room. Supposedly a space heater had caused it. I could see out the window that my mom was trying to focus on her conversation but was too distracted by the apartment. She kept looking back at us. She knew I was at the window, hypnotized by the lights flashing on the fire trucks. I still have a vivid picture in my mind of the front room window, busted open and pitch black. My mom called my grandpa and my uncle. So many family members showed up that night.

We cried and were comforted. Soon it was time to leave. I did not want to go. I saw so many of our belongings in the backyard and on the side of the building. A friend was going to go back in later and see if anything could be recovered. I was heartbroken. We lived with my grandma until we found a new home.

I live with this memory every day. It always makes me nervous, and sometimes it makes me cry. However, it was just another obstacle in my life, and the way I have overcome it has changed me. I am stronger than I thought I could ever be. I have learned how to ignore the small stuff; I don't worry as much about fights over nothing, or having to do something I really don't want to, or not getting my way, or guys, or problems with friends. I learned to be strong. If one thing goes wrong, or if one event turns out badly, it is not the end of the world. Like I have always been told, "What doesn't kill you makes you stronger." Thinking about it all, this is what came to me—even though I only really hear that line when I am being told to clean my room. However, just like my world wasn't over when I had to clean my room, life went on after my apartment burned down.

Luckily, I didn't lose everything. We did preserve a couple things: A box of pictures and a laundry bag full of my mom's clothes were still okay. Some video tapes were still good, too. I was most thankful, though, for the pictures. A picture can speak a thousand words. I also learned that family is always going to be worth more than a house, material things, and wealth. So many things happened in that first little apartment—all white, almost all carpet, with a small, crowded attic. I miss the pictures on the walls. My bedroom in the back was the most fun part of the house.

However, even though our new apartment is so different—much bigger and better, in many ways—I still miss the old one. Those things that happened are memories. I hope to never forget.

WHAT HAPPENS

Angelica Troche

What happens
What happens when you love someone
But you can't be with them?
You cry and sob.
What happens when you think about
That person and cry for them?
You end up only hurting yourself.
What happens when you want to be
Held by that person but you can't be?
You find someone else to comfort you.
What happens when you miss them
But you can't see them?
You suffer while you wait.

What happens when you feel
You can't live without them?
You spend every minute of the day
Worrying about what will happen next.
And then what happens when you find
That they don't feel the same way?
You try to move on,
When inside you know you can't.

You are still waiting.

ABOUT ASPIRA

ABOUT THE TEACHER

Ms. Leslie Lockett grew up in St. Louis, Missouri, and has been teaching English in Chicago Public Schools for four years. Currently in her first year at Aspira, she teaches Humanities and College Literacy, spending between two and a half and three hours per day with each of her two groups of students—who, in addition to being exceptionally smart and talented, are by far the funniest she has ever met. Her parakeet's first name is Pickle.

ABOUT THE SCHOOL

ASPIRA Early College High School (AEC) opened its doors for the first time this school year. It was housed at Haugan Middle School throughout the book project with 826CHI, before moving to its new building at 3986 West Barry Avenue in Chicago. AEC's mission is to provide a high quality secondary education leading to a high school diploma and dual-enrollment/early college opportunities for Chicago's at-risk youth. It is the first early college high school in Illinois partnered with a four-year university, Northeastern Illinois University. The early college model is based on the theory that students are more likely to succeed in higher education if they have been exposed to college classes while attending high school. The students begin taking classes at Northeastern University during their junior year, with the idea that they will graduate high school with at least one year of college credit under their belts. Rather than the standard practice of dual enrollment, AEC's students carefully plan a sequence of college courses so they can take care of their general educational requirements early and focus on their major as soon as they enter college full-time. While at school, students stay with the same group of students every class period, traveling from class to class together. Spending a significant amount of time together and with their teachers encourages close relationships between the students and their teachers. Each group is named after a university, fostering student identity within the group and further promoting the theme of college readiness.

ABOUT 826CHI

826CHI is a non-profit organization dedicated to supporting students ages six to eighteen with their creative and expository writing skills, and to helping teachers inspire their students to write. Our services are structured around the understanding that great leaps in learning can happen with one-on-one attention, and that strong writing skills are fundamental to future success.

826CHI provides drop-in tutoring, class field trips, writing workshops, and in-schools programs—all free of charge—for students, classes, and schools. All of our programs are challenging and enjoyable, and ultimately strengthen each student's power to express ideas effectively, creatively, confidently, and in his or her individual voice.

Driving our mission home are more than five hundred volunteers—
the professional writers, teachers and artists, to name a few, who staff each
and every program 826CHI offers, enabling us to serve five thousand
students annually.

* * *

Our Programs

826CHI programs reach students at every opportunity—in school, after
school, in the evenings, and on weekends.

TUTUORING

826CHI's site is packed four afternoons a week with students who come
in for free one-on-one tutoring after school. We serve students of all skill
levels and interests, most of whom live or go to school within walking
distance of our writing center. Literacy is stressed through daily reading
and monthly chapbook projects, where students' writing around a particular theme is compiled into small books. Pre-registration is not
required, and students are welcome to show up any school day, Monday
through Thursday, from 3:00 until 5:30 p.m.

FIELD TRIPS

826CHI invites teachers to bring their students to our site through our
field trip program. Teachers may choose from several field trip formats
depending on their interests and grade level. The most popular field trip
is an 826-original project, called Storytelling & Bookmaking, in which

students write, illustrate, and bind their own books within a two-hour period. The field trip program is so popular that our schedule is filled almost a year in advance. To join our educator e-mail list to be notified when our registration for the next school year opens up, please visit our Web site at www.826chi.org.

IN-SCHOOLS

It is not feasible for all classes to come to us, so we dispatch teams of volunteers into local schools. At a teacher's behest, we will send tutors into classrooms around the city to provide one-on-one assistance to students as they tackle various projects—Young Authors books, research papers, oral histories, basic writing assignments, and college entrance essays. If you are a teacher interested in inviting our tutors into your classroom, please contact us through our Web site.

WORKSHOPS

826CHI offers free workshops that provide in-depth writing instruction in a variety of areas that schools often cannot include in their curriculum, such as cartooning, bookmaking, playwriting, zine-making, or college entrance essay writing. All workshops are project-based and are taught by experienced, accomplished volunteers. Connecting Chicago students with these creative and generous mentors allows students to dream and achieve on a grand scale. Please visit our Web site to view our current workshop schedule.

STUDENT PUBLISHING

At 826CHI, we know the quality of student work is greatly enhanced when it is shared with an authentic audience, so we are committed to publishing student work, whether it be in small chapbooks that we bind in-house, or in professionally published volumes, such as this one. All forms of student publishing are available for purchase at The Boring Store.

* * *

The Boring Store

826CHI shares its space with The Boring Store, Chicago's only under-cover secret agent supply store. We have grappling hooks, envelope x-ray spray, and an ever-expanding array of fake moustaches. We also have heavy surveillance at the door. All proceeds from The Boring Store go directly toward supporting 826CHI's programs for Chicago students.

Please visit us online at www.826chi.org or in person at 1331 North Milwaukee Avenue in Wicker Park to learn more about our programs and to find out how you can get involved.